CREATIVE CRAFTS

APPLIQUÉ
IDEAS

CREATIVE CRAFTS

APPLIQUÉ IDEAS

Hedi Probst-Reinhardt

STACKPOLE BOOKS

Contents

Foreword

Do you want to learn a creative craft that will give you pleasure and teach you how to transform clothing and soft furnishings into something special? Then this is the book for you. Phone your friends and invite them to a 'Make and mend coffee session'. Get them to bring old sweaters, dresses, children's clothes or fabric remnants and put your heads together to see what you can turn these into. You might think it would be impossible to come up with anything of any use. Don't worry – once you start talking you will find ideas beginning to take shape. To supplement these you will also find a wide range of ideas in this book. I hope it will show you how you can be creative even if you think you are not that good with your hands!

You think you can't sew? That's no reason to give up. Try working with a group of friends and you will usually find that your talents complement each other. And if you

prefer to work by yourself, I can show you how to set about it – for this book will teach you all the techniques you need to make any of the items included. I hope you will feel encouraged to develop your own ideas from the easy-to-make designs that I have chosen. The many examples included in this book are simply intended to get you started.

In the hope of appealing to as wide a range of readers as possible I have included both simple and difficult appliqué designs. The book begins by taking a look at the range and variation of appliqué. Then the basic techniques are explained, followed by a collection of designs which I hope will inspire many ideas for both clothes and soft-furnishings. It has not always been possible to provide detailed instructions here, for many of the measurements and techniques in appliqué work depend on your choice of fabrics. Finally, a collection of works by fabric artists

illustrate the original ways in which different fabrics and threads can be used. Don't be overawed by this picture gallery, for you have yet to discover what you yourself can do.

Why not start today! I wish you every happiness and success in your work.

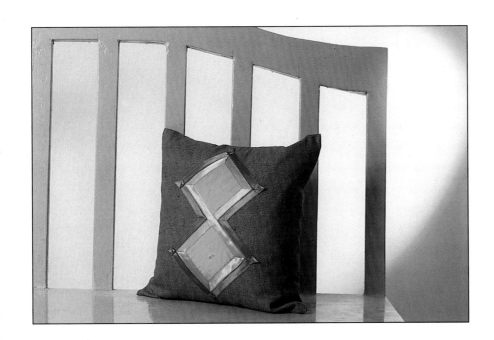

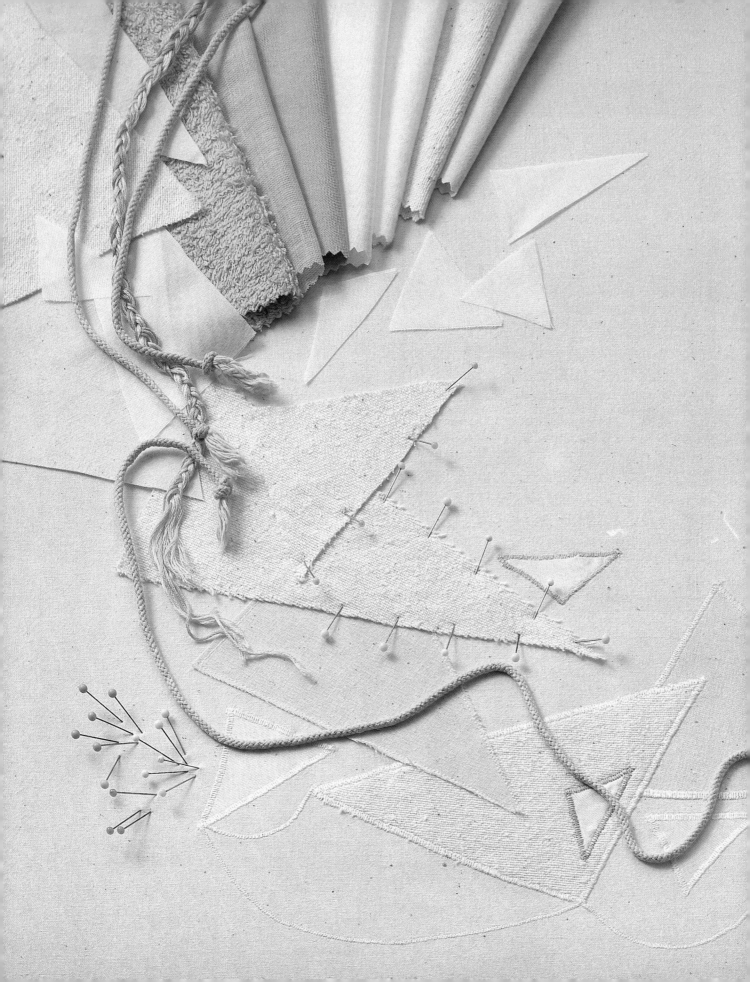

What is Appliqué?

Simple but effective

Basically appliqué means to place something against a background and to secure it in place. In the area of textiles, for example, this means the decorating of a fabric by the sewing on of a design in textile or some other material. In the strictest sense of the word, patch pockets on a coat or designer labels on jeans are in fact appliqué. Simple as the idea may sound, it offers endless possibilities. The most important aspect of appliqué is the choice of materials, followed by the design of the motif, the choice of colour scheme and the sewing method, whether for instance it is to be hand or machine stitched.

If one were to attempt to categorise appliqué within the complete system of textile techniques, one would have to include it with the surface-decorating techniques. (In contrast, crochet and weaving are surface-forming techniques, for these produce a fabric which is then worked further.) The basic prerequisite of appliqué is a background fabric (woven or knitted, felt, fur or leather, for example) which can be decorated with additional materials. Appliqué is a similar process to embroidery, for here, too, one works with

appropriate materials (in this case threads of varying textures and colours) to decorate a background fabric. In both processes the type of stitch chosen is an important factor in the effectiveness of the motif.

The transition from embroidery to appliqué is in fact a smooth one. If, for instance, one chooses to embroider with extremely thick thread in the form of cord, braid or ribbon, it clearly is impossible simply to pull it through the fabric by means of a needle as one would with an embroidery thread. The problem can be solved in the following way. The cord, thread or ribbon which is to be used for surface decoration is simply laid in place on the surface of the fabric and is usually stitched into place with invisible stitches which will not detract from the design.

In the monasteries of old, costly materials such as gold thread were worked in this way. It was considered a waste to continually bring the thread through to the wrong side of the fabric where it could not be seen. Instead it was sewn in close-set rows to the background material to create whole areas. Basically this so-called 'laying-on' technique was a form of appliqué.

Taking things one step further it was possible to decorate large areas more easily by simply sewing on pieces of fabric of the size, shape and colour required, thus cutting down on the time-consuming sewing required. Additional decoration, or small details of a pictorial design, for instance, are still provided in the form of embroidery.

Naturally it is possible to appliqué with other textile materials (feathers, unspun wool, raffia, for example) and other non-textile materials (beads, stones, shells, wire, sequins, pieces of glass and metal). There are no limits to the imagination. It is important, however, to think about how the article is to be used, for instance, as an article of clothing that will need regular washing, or as a picture, cushion cover, oven-glove or an original greetings card!

Naturally, I could fill a number of volumes with all that I would like to be able to say or to show you. The important thing here, however, has been to provide an introduction to the subject and to encourage you to try it for yourself, for no book can be a substitute for the pleasure of doing something for yourself, of achieving your first success or of handling for yourself these fascinating materials.

Think carefully about the fabric that is to form the background for your design. It offers you the opportunity to create a lively relief-effect. You will find you are continually able to come up with new ideas when you look at the various materials available and try them out in different combinations. Be bold and try occasionally to forget your fixed ideas about shape and colour. For it is certainly true that practical experience and experimenting are better than any amount of study.

Many possible uses

It is of course an entirely individual matter whether you have little previous sewing experience and want to make a simple but effective, inexpensive item, or whether you want to put a lot of planning, patience and sewing experience into creating a real work of art. Anything is possible with this technique which can be geared to your own ambitions and abilities.

One particular advantage of decorative textile techniques is that they can be used in so many different areas. They are by no means restricted to turning out pictures for the wall, for in theory any everyday textile article can be given a new look by means of appliqué. The areas of fashion and soft-furnishings are rich in opportunities. Here it is often small, but cleverly worked, details which catch the attention and create the most effect. It takes relatively little time to brighten up some boring item of clothing with a cleverly designed appliqué motif. In the

home you can use appliqué on curtains, for instance, on cushion covers, tablecloths and matching napkins. Even mirror frames and lampshades can be decorated with appliqué. Always bear in mind, however, the overall harmony of a room. A decorative wall picture can create a focal point for a room when you combine imagination with the demands set by the colour and style of the room in which it is to be hung. Appliquéd bookcovers make charmingly old-fashioned presents for close friends.

Appliqué also makes an effective form of decoration in the kitchen. An appliquéd motif on a plain apron, original oven-gloves or tray-cloth, or a picture of fruit and vegetables can give the room an atmosphere all of its own.

In the bedroom, appliqué can turn

a plain, shop-bought bedspread into an individual accessory. A cushion with the same design completes the picture. Similarly you can use matching designs to personalise bath-robes, hand and bath-towels or bath-mats.

The best way of expressing your personality through appliqué is to decorate items of clothing such as coats, sweaters, scarves, shirts, jackets, dresses and T-shirts. In children's clothes you can use appliqué to give a new look to hand-me-downs. I could go on, but I do not want to stand in the way of your own creativity. You know your own home better than anyone else and you know better than anyone else which items in your wardrobe are old-fashioned but too good to throw out and could do with a facelift to get you wearing them again.

A lively appliqué design in ribbon and cord on a plain velour sweatshirt.

All over the world

The urge to decorate oneself and one's surroundings is common to mankind throughout the world. In all the varied forms of decoration in all aspects of life, including the area of textiles, we are struck not only by the taste, the feeling for shape and colour, and the individuality of the separate designs, but also by the way that textile design is embedded in the traditions of each separate culture. It is not my intention to cover all the appliqué techniques of different nationalities and of different periods of history in a few short pages, but rather to present a small cross-section in words and pictures which I hope will encourage you to look into it more closely when you come across unusual appliqué designs, both old and modern. Perhaps you will feel encouraged to try and copy some of these techniques or to try out these beautiful colours and motifs.

Appliqué of the North American settlers

In the 18th and 19th centuries the settlers in North America developed patchwork into a true folk art. As the word implies this was an art using small scraps of fabric and was used mainly for bedcovers. Since the top, bottom and padded lining of the cover were held together and at the same time decorated with quilting stitches, these covers were known as quilts. One specialised form of this was the appliquéd quilt, where appliqué was often combined with patchwork. Patchwork and much appliqué work were based on geometric shapes. Appliqué motifs can, for example, be made up using the patchwork technique and then sewn on to the separate elements of the patchwork cover, or appliqué can be made to resemble patchwork.

The appliqué technique, however, allowed much greater freedom: contours could be much more varied, separate sections could be brought out or made to recede simply by overlapping, and detailed work became possible.

These styles of textile work were the product of necessity. In the 18th century, textiles had to be transported over long distances, making them expensive and difficult to come by. So the settlers valued any scraps of fabric which still had some use in them and joined them together to make new pieces of fabric. In this way necessity produced a new technique which is still practised today and which (in different parts of the world) still produces highly varied and extremely artistic work.

Richly decorated ceremonial dress of the Bedouin women of the area south of Jaffa.

10

'Bird of Paradise' bedcover. This American bridal quilt was made in the
Albany, New York area, around 1858/63. (Museum of American Folk Art, New York)

The Mola technique of the Indians

Mola appliqué was developed into a folk art by the women of the Cuña Indians who live on the San Blas Islands off the coast of Panama. The Cuñas have remained largely un-influenced by the outside world so that this folk art has continued to develop right up to the present day.

The impact of the dress of European settlers brought them to transfer the motifs used in their body painting to decorate their traditional dress and to the women's blouses in particular. A black line painted from the forehead down the nose is all that remains today of the original body painting.

On the Molas one finds mainly brightly coloured representations of animals and plants, mythological motifs and ornamental designs. Cuña Molas are produced with extremely simple tools, but their imaginative designs and the originality of their forms and colours has made them popular with art collectors.

Molas are made as follows: two or more layers of colour-contrasting fabric, usually fine cotton, are laid one on top of the other and sewn together at the edges. Beginning with the top layer, the shape of the motif is now cut out and the edges of each shape sewn by hand to the layer beneath. Each cut reveals the colour of the next layer of fabric. Larger motifs are cut in the top layer than in the underlying layers so that a brightly coloured, stepped effect is produced. The motif is worked in

this way from the top downwards. This method is also known as 'reverse appliqué'.

The Cuñas also place additional smaller pieces of fabric between the separate layers and work them in the same way. This allows for extra colours without the need for an entire extra layer of fabric. This is the method used to add an extra splash of colour at the centre of the design. Lines too fine to be appliquéd are simply embroidered on with matching thread.

These Molas are highly valued for the harmony of their forms and their well-balanced colouring, which is normally extremely bright. Often one finds the same designs on the reverse side of the blouses, the same cut-out technique being used again here.

Above: *A Samurai's coat of arms was depicted on a padded battledress. Late 18th century, Japan. (Private collection)*

Above: *Ceremonial robe of the South American Indians with appliquéd feathers and parrot skin. Ecuador. (Stummer Collection, Munich)*

Hawaii

English missionaries taught the women of Hawaii to make quilts from small scraps of fabric. Inspired by the natural forms amongst which they lived, such as pineapples, breadfruit and figs, as well as by mythological subjects, they developed their own stock of motifs which they reproduced mainly in appliqué. The resulting garlands of designs, so typical of the island, are called 'leis'. They are bright red on a white background. Bright green on a white background is popular for floral motifs. Red and yellow, the royal colours, are found principally on the large quilted bedcovers which are normally decorated with a single intricate appliqué motif cut from one piece of fabric. Consecutive lines of quilting follow the outline of the motif, and these have a decorative effect as well as a functional one of holding the layers of fabric and the padding together.

Afghanistan

The appliqué work of eastern Afghanistan is known as 'Gul'. Worked on cotton, the central motif consists of a rosette of beads surrounded by rows of beads of varying diameter. These appliqué designs in black, dark blue or plum-coloured beads are used to decorate clothing. The spirals around the rosette are usually white, light blue or turquoise in colour. Often this form of appliqué is used in combination with embroidery and small mirrors. The overall design has an air of richness about it and shows great attention to detail. The main element in the design is the circle.

Hungary

In Hungary both the Ködmön, the traditional sheepskin waistcoats worn by Hungarian women and girls, and the Szür, the coats worn by young men when they go courting for a wife, are decorated with appliqué. In addition to the appliqué on clothing, tulle is richly appliquéd with linen designs. This is used mainly for table linen which is beautifully and lovingly worked.

Siberia

The Ghiliak tribe in south-eastern Siberia uses the skin of the highly valued Koumza salmon to make intricate appliqués on bridal clothes. A favourite motif for these important garments is the tree of life carried by birds, which is a symbol of fertility.

India and Pakistan

A special feature of many forms of Indian appliqué work are the small mirrors attached to the fabric by a circle of embroidery. This mirror appliqué work, most of which comes from Pakistan, is known as 'Shishadur'. The mirrors, which originally contained a small piece of silver and were blown by mouth, are said to keep evil spirits at bay. Nowadays manufactured mirror glass or mica is used, fixed in place with cross-stitch and then sewn around with a decorative stitch in a contrasting colour.

Romania

Appliqué on coats and the 'cojocele', or waistcoats, takes the form of punched leather, combined here and there with mirrorwork.

Minister. Part of a religious dancing robe from Tibet, 19th century. (University of Zurich, Ethnology collection)

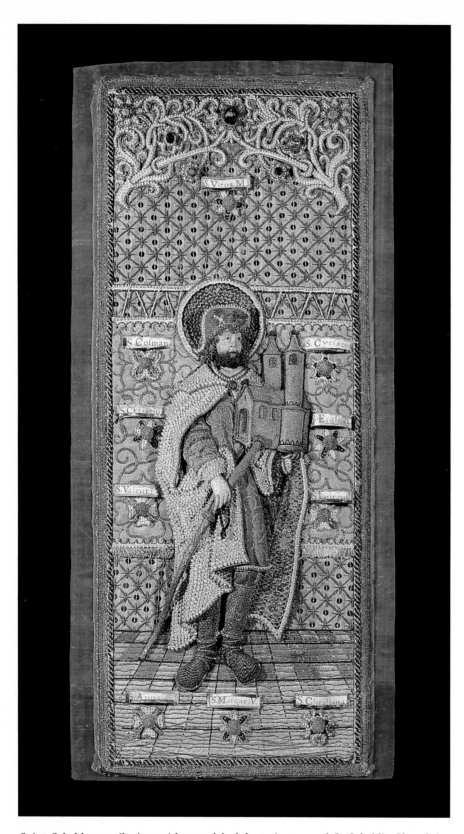

Saint Sebald as a pilgrim, with a model of the twin-towered St Sebald's Church in Nuremberg, Germany, around 1519. (Bayerisches Nationalmuseum, Munich)

France

The appliqué techniques practised in France go back to the Middle Ages. Fabric was glued to thin paper and then pressed. When dry the motif was cut out, again glued and fixed to the background with simple stitches. A thin cord was laid around the edges and stitched invisibly into place.

Austria

In Austria, generations of master scythe-makers succeeded in integrating much of their peasant culture into their increasingly middle-class way of life. Clothing played an important part in the process and women's dress of the time is worthy of mention as an example of the way a basic craft was developed. The brown dirndl skirt, the gold Linz cap and the champagne-coloured silk apron covered with embroidery and appliqué are all signs of the increased wealth and sophistication of these people.

14

Germany

Wall coverings using an old appliqué technique are a feature of the 17th and 18th centuries. These were made chiefly in Germany and Austria. The basic materials used were silk fabrics and ribbons which, following a preliminary drawing, were glued behind the cut-outs of a cardboard stencil. The solid parts of the stencil corresponded to the outline and inner detail of the motif. The stencil with the fabric glued to it was then placed on the background material and held in place by over-sewing the remaining sections of stencil. Additional decoration was often provided by metal foil and sequins.

During the Middle Ages a rich treasury of textile works of art were created. While many works in the Christian tradition were destroyed by iconoclasm, war and secularisation, thankfully many of these treasures survived in churches and monasteries.

Appliqué and embroidery techniques were often used to complement one another while beads, gems, metals and metallic threads were used to create a relief effect and to add richness to the work.

Fragment of a wall covering from the Bayerisches Kabinett in Koblenz Castle, Munich, Germany, 1784–86. (Residence, Munich, Reserve collection)

Materials and equipment

Appliqué work actually begins with the collecting together of a variety of materials. Imaginative ideas usually develop at this early stage for the senses of colour and touch play an important part in selecting materials. Often it is better to let the materials themselves inspire your design than to work with too fixed an idea of the finished work! The disappointment of not being able to find just what you want can often make you abandon your project altogether.

Naturally not every material is suitable for every purpose and your choice of material will often depend on the type of object it is to decorate. This section will give you a few tips on this.

The type of material also determines which appliqué method should be used, be it hand-sewing (with invisible or decorative stitches) or machine-sewing. You will probably have all the equipment you need to hand at home, but the list on page 21 will show you if there is anything you need to buy specially.

Choosing materials

If you feel like trying your hand at appliqué work, it is not a good idea to plan your work and then to rush out in search of suitable materials. It is much better and more interesting if you already have a small collection of materials that you can use. The wider the variety of materials you have to hand, the easier it will be to come up with an original idea for your work. Keep a remnant bag for

Colour and texture are important when choosing appropriate materials.

left-over fabrics and remember that your wardrobe can provide a rich source of materials. Don't send everything straight off to the jumble sale as soon as it goes out of fashion. Hang on to those old dresses, jackets, sweaters and T-shirts which may have shrunk or faded; lacy petticoats that have become too short; shirts and blouses with old-fashioned collars; old ties and outgrown children's clothes. Curtains from the old house can be put to a new use, remnants of a pretty summer fabric can still be used, and those crocheted or knitted fragments in your work basket – they may never make a cardigan, but perhaps they will do to decorate another sweater.

Even if you have none of these, that is no reason to ignore your creative drive. Take yourself off on a fabric safari! Go around the flea markets and charity shops looking for old lace and braid, for lace doilies or curtains, for fabric offcuts and scarves. Phone your friends and relations and ask them if they have old things that they no longer want. They will be glad to help for it will encourage them to clear out their wardrobes knowing that the clothing they no longer want will be appreciated by someone else.

Even if you don't like going to the sales, it can be worth making the effort. You are bound to find some inexpensive article of clothing which you can turn into something special with appliqué, or some interesting fabric remnants.

Furniture makers sometimes have clearance sales of fabric samples. Don't miss the opportunity if it arises, for furnishing fabrics are extremely attractive and have many uses. Often an upholsterer will let you have remnants very cheaply. It is worth asking.

In addition, furriers will sometimes let you have fur remnants which make eye-catching decorations. You can get leather remnants and offcuts very cheaply from leather factories or handicraft shops.

And if there is some specific material that you just can't find, why not put an advertisement in the local paper. I have uncovered hand-made lace, small doilies, old braid and even a beautiful hand-made christening robe simply by advertising.

A collection of a wide variety of materials which can be used in appliqué work.

All you need to know about materials

It is impossible for me to describe in detail every type of material that you could possibly use. When you think how many different types of fabrics there are, you will see that I can only concentrate on the main ones. Nevertheless I hope to be able to broaden your outlook a little, for it would be limiting your creative potential to restrict your appliqué work to merely sewing on pieces of fabric.

One of the most important questions to consider in selecting materials is whether the appliqué is to be functional or decorative. It may seem as if I am splitting hairs here, for a functional appliqué, like that on a bath-towel for instance, is also decorative, and an appliqué picture which hangs on the wall is also functional – serving as a room decoration. What I mean in making this distinction is that one must differentiate between things that will be used or worn and will need regular washing and those that will remain undisturbed.

Functional appliqué (like that on cardigans, T-shirts or bath-towels) requires materials that are washable and colour-fast and that will not shrink or fray. It is a good idea to wash and iron all materials before using them. After washing, pin crumpled lace onto a thick piece of fabric to dry. Old white materials which have turned yellow with age should be bleached carefully before use.

Patterned or plain – any fabric can be used for appliqué, but bear in mind the purpose for which it is to be used.

Fabrics

Fabrics are found in most appliqué work, for the background at least is generally fabric. Remember that large format designs can take a thicker fabric than small ones.

In deciding which materials to use, personal taste is of course the most important factor. This makes it impossible to give any fixed, irrefutable rules. But there are several things that you should bear in mind.

Woven fabrics keep their shape better than knitted ones, which can easily go out of shape as you work with them. You can often spoil a design by combining materials that are too thick with very fine ones.

You can use either plain or patterned fabrics in appliqué work. If the pattern is very small you can cut the fabric without worrying about the pattern. With larger patterns you will have to take account of the effect of the pattern on the overall design when cutting the fabric. With many fabrics it is possible to cut out individual motifs (with furnishing fabric for instance) and to use the whole motif (see cushion, page 42).

When using plain fabrics the impact of the design comes from clever use of colour. If you have a large collection of fabrics to choose from you can create subtle designs with different shades of the same colour. Contrasting colours, on the other hand, produce more striking effects. (Plain fabrics are particularly effective for appliqué.)

If you want to create transparent or depth effects you can finish off with transparent fabrics.

Cotton This is one of the most popular materials. Cotton fabrics include muslin, cambric, cretonne, poplin, chintz, seersucker and piqué. These fabrics are excellent for appliqué as they will not go out of shape and are relatively crease-resistant. They are not inclined to fray as they are usually closely woven. You can buy cotton fabrics in various qualities and colours and they are relatively inexpensive. They generally tend to shrink more in one direction than the other so it is a good idea to wash and iron them before use to avoid them shrinking later.

Linens These and similar mixed weaves make excellent backgrounds for appliqué. Because of its fairly loose weave linen is best used for decorative purposes. If used for functional articles there is a danger that it might go out of shape or fray.

Woollens In principle, woollen fabrics can also be used, although their natural elasticity makes them rather difficult to work with. You should also bear in mind that pure wool requires much more careful washing than cotton, which is easy to wash. You should pay particular attention to this when combining a number of materials in one pattern.

Silk This is the most luxurious fabric of all and is available in many beautiful colours and patterns, but it is a delicate fabric that needs extremely careful handling. Turned edges (hems) will show through fine silk fabrics, so where necessary make sure you keep your hems absolutely even. You also need to take care when ironing silk; the creases will come out better if you iron it damp. A lining will make silk appliqué stronger. (Before attempting silk appliqué it is best to have some experience of other flimsy fabrics.)

Velvet Fabrics with a deep nap include velvet and corduroy, a special form of velvet. When using these fabrics pay attention to the direction the nap lies, for it shades either light or dark in the light depending on the lie of the nap. The linear structure of corduroy makes it ideal for geometric or highly simplified designs. It is also useful in a landscape, for example, to give the effect of a ploughed field. Velvet is a delicate material and is not easy to work

with. It should always be ironed extremely carefully using a damp cloth on the wrong side.

Felt On the other hand, felt is excellent for the beginner. It is not a woven material made of separate threads but is made by compressing fibres together, so it is guaranteed not to fray and need not be hemmed. It is available in a number of striking colours and is excellent for wall decorations, especially for poster-type appliqués for a child's room. You should not use felt, however, for articles that will be worn a lot and need frequent washing for it will not withstand regular washing.

Lamé and brocade These two patterned fabrics, usually with metallic effects, are often used for evening dresses. They will add a touch of glamour to any appliqué design. Brocade, including furnishing brocade, gains its effect from its raised pattern. It can be used in interesting ways in appliqué pictures. You should always use an extremely strong background for these fabrics.

Satin (often made from cotton or viscose) This has a tight, smooth weave. Like silk, it is available in the most subtle shades. Since it tends to crease it needs careful handling. It is excellent for fine appliqué work.

Lining fabrics These are also available in a wide variety of colours. They are similar to satin, but have a slightly different weave which makes them less shiny.

Lace All kinds of lace – be it in a man-made fibre, expensive bobbin lace in linen, or crocheted cotton lace – gives any article onto which it is sewn an air of lightness and nostalgia. You can buy lace fabrics and braid by the metre, but equally well you can use small lace doilies, bits of lace curtain and so on. If you want to match a piece of lace to the other fabrics used in your appliqué design it is very easy to dye. (However man-made fibres do not dye well.)

Leather (or suede) is now available in a range of beautiful colours. It is highly effective in combination with linen fabrics or strongly textured

brocade. You should use a special leather needle to sew it or, if you are using a sewing machine, there is a special foot you can attach for leatherwork. (Use a size 80 needle.) You can smooth creases from leather with a steam iron. To do this, place the leather under a dry linen cloth and use the iron on the wool setting.

Fur Pieces of fur can be used to form an eye-catching decoration on leather clothes or thick outerwear, for such materials do not need to be washed regularly. Like leather, fur should be sewn to the background with a strong needle.

Plain, light-coloured fabrics show off the structure of the fabric.

Ribbons, braids and cords

Fabrics used for appliqué determine the colour of the work, while form is created by the cutting of the fabric to make the outlines of the various areas.

A different effect is achieved, however, with appliquéd ribbons and braids, with cords, trimmings, gift-wrap ribbon, webbing or with bias binding. All of these can be used to form striking line effects. There is no reason why you should not make an entire appliqué design from ribbons and cords, but they are more often used to trim a basic fabric appliqué and add emphasis to outlines. Used on their own they can create interesting graphic effects.

They are effective not only in breaking up large areas of plain fabric, but are often eye-catching in the way that they stand up in relief from the background fabric.

Unspun fibres

An interesting approach is to go back a step further and use textile materials in their original form.

All types of fibres are suitable for appliqué, including raw wool (available in a range of colours), cotton-wool, raffia, sisal, hemp or polyester fibre.

You can also untwist interesting knitting wools or unravel fabric and use these fibres. Bear in mind that, because of their loose composition, such materials will not take wear and tear, and only use them in decorative items where they will not be subjected to daily use.

Non-textile materials

This includes anything that can be fixed in some way with needle and thread to an appliqué background. (Buttons can be included among non-textile appliqué materials even though they may or may not be purely for decoration.)

I could begin my list with sequins, beads, feathers, buttons, toggles and corks and finish it with curtain rings, fishing tackle, buckles, shells and gems, and still leave plenty of scope for your imagination, for the list could go on endlessly.

Remember though, that not everything will wash. To ensure that all your work is not ruined, keep these more unusual things for decorative appliqué work or make sure that they can be easily removed for washing.

One further point: do not overdo the use of striking or unusual items, for it is easy to make a design too fussy or to lose sight of the fact that it is a textile decoration that one is producing. Unless, of course, you are actually trying to make a collage from contrasting materials.

Sewing thread

It is up to you to decide whether you will hand or machine sew the sections of appliqué into place. You must also decide whether you prefer an invisible stitch or whether the stitch itself is to form an element in the overall design. If you choose to make the stitching part of the design, this can be done, for example, with a large but close-set zig-zag stitch or with blanket stitch. Basically, any sewing or embroidery thread can be used. The colour and thickness of the thread will depend on the effect you want to achieve and on the other materials used. Top-stitching around the edges of appliqué fabric pieces in a contrasting colour can, for instance, add life to a design of subdued colour.

Equipment and accessories

In appliqué we have to distinguish between two important stages of work. The first includes the designing and the transfer of the design to the fabric, the other is the appliqué itself.

If you put as much time and effort into the preparatory stages as into making the appliqué, your finished design will be much more pleasing. Never be tempted to rush into things and cut fabric freehand. As a rule this will only make extra work in the end (shapes and sizes may be wrongly estimated) and result in wasted material.

A review of the materials you will need for both the designing and sewing stages. You will already have most of these around the house.

Aids to design and transfer of motif
Paper (ordinary writing or drawing paper) for both sketching and designing.
Graph paper for precise drawing of geometric shapes.
Tracing paper for copying motifs.
Cardboard from which to cut the templates.
Pencil, felt-tip or ball-pen for designing or tracing motifs.
Felt-tips or watercolours for designing your colour schemes.
Dressmaking chalk or iron-on pen to mark motif on fabric.
Ruler, measuring tape (and compass) to measure fabric and draw accurate outlines (both long and short rulers).
Scissors (paper and dressmaking) to cut templates and fabric. Always remember that different scissors are used for different tasks. They should be sharp and also comfortable to use. Paper will blunt fabric scissors.

Pins to temporarily hold templates, iron-on backing and fabric pieces in place.
Iron-on backing (one or two-sided adhesive) to reinforce fabric pieces.
Iron to iron fabric after completing each stage and to iron on backing.

Equipment for sewing appliqué
Pins and basting thread to sew sections or hems.
Sewing or embroidery needles to baste and sew sections in place, in sizes to suit thread used.
Sewing machine with appropriate-sized needle and with leatherwork foot where necessary. The choice of sewing machine is, of course, one of the most important decisions a needlewoman will ever make.
Sewing or embroidery thread (or other thread) for final hand or machine sewing.
Scissors to trim edges and cut thread.

Appliqué techniques

Just as there are many possibilities in the choice of materials, there is no hard and fast rule about the way appliqué should be sewn. However, the sewing method contributes to the overall effect, so it is important to choose the most effective method. It is beyond the scope of this book to describe all the possible variations, so I will concentrate on a selection of the main stitches. The first thing to be decided is whether you intend to hand or machine sew. Machined seams are usually stronger and take less time, but hand sewing offers more freedom, especially if you want to use a decorative stitch.

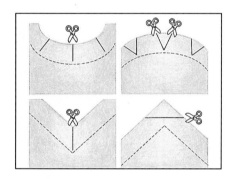

Appliquéing by hand

If you decide to hand sew your appliqué, you must consider whether the stitches are to be invisible or to contribute to the design. Here are a few of the many possibilities open to you.

Hemming stitch
This is used when you do not want the stitches to be seen and when you do not wish to emphasise the edges of the fabric. But you can also use it when you intend to emphasise the motif by outlining it with a length of cord.

Use a matching thread, not too thick, and try to keep the stitches even. When using hemming stitch you will first need to turn under a small hem of about 4 mm/⅛ in to prevent the fabric fraying. The final effect will be neater if the hem is turned under and iron or basted into position before you appliqué it.

You will need to treat curved edges and corners in the following way to ensure that the hem lies flat: For the inside of a curve, snip the edge of the fabric several times to just short of the sewing line. For the outside of a curve, cut out small triangles to prevent creases in the seam. Inside corners should also be snipped to just short of the seam line; for outside corners cut off the point of the corner (see diagram left).

Decorative stitches
If you leaf through handicraft books and magazines you will find a number of embroidery stitches that can be used for appliqué. They not only hold the fabric firmly to the background but also decorate the edges. But be careful! It is all too easy to overemphasise the edges and make the work look fussy. Think carefully about which thread and stitch you are going to use, for the choice is endless.

It can be effective if the embroidery stitch is repeated somewhere else on the work, so that it not only holds the appliqué in place but also forms a link between the appliqué and the background fabric and gives the work a unified appearance which will be pleasing to the eye.

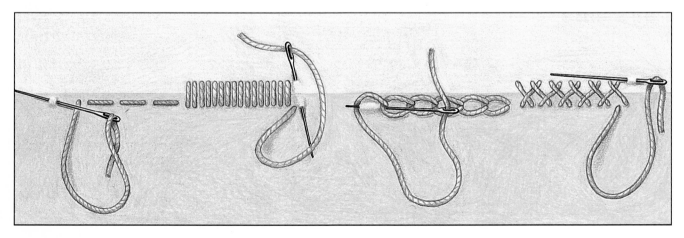

Useful decorative stitches:
running stitch, satin stitch, chain stitch, herringbone stitch (from left to right).

If I describe just a few stitches for you, it may revive memories of your school sewing classes or lead you on to learn more about the numerous stitches available.

Running stitch This is the best stitch for simple decorations. Stitch (not too close to the edge) at very short intervals (about 2 mm/¹⁄₁₀ in) through both layers of fabric. If you want a frayed-edge effect, remember it is not necessary to turn under a hem.

Satin stitch (also known as straight stitch) This is one of the most popular stitches for appliqué because it conceals cut edges extremely well. Stitches should be even and made close together perpendicular to the edge of the fabric. When stitches of varying length are used close together, this is known as graduated satin stitch. It can be used on curves or corners.

If you begin by sewing several rows of running stitch along the edge of the fabric this serves as a kind of padding for the satin stitch. It gives the edging solidity and extra emphasis. You can also achieve the same effect by using a bulky thread (wool for instance).

Chain stitch This too can emphasise contours in an interesting way. To keep it even, the distance between the point where the needle goes in and where it comes out must be kept exactly the same. The chain is formed while the needle is in the material by bringing the thread under the point of the needle. Then the needle is pulled through and you are ready to make the next link in the chain by inserting the point of the needle exactly next to the point where it last came out, that is, inside the previous link of the chain. The chain is made by repeating just this one stitch. When you come to the end of the 'chain', insert the needle through the material just outside the last link, instead of inside, but still directly next to the hole where it last emerged. This holds the final loop in place.

Herringbone stitch This also gives a strong emphasis to the contours for, with its criss-crossing lines, it has quite an eye-catching structure. If you are clever enough to work it into the overall design it can be highly effective. It is excellent for large decorative appliqué works.

The stitch is easier than it looks. Always stitching in the same direction, make small stitches parallel to the edge, above and below the edge alternately, that is, first through the background fabric and next through the piece of appliqué. Work from left to right with stitches sewn from right to left if you are right-handed, or vice versa if you are left-handed. The threads will then cross automatically on the front of the fabric.

Sewing on sequins
To make single sequins particularly eye-catching, use tiny beads in a matching shade. Bring your needle and thread up through the fabric, through the middle of the sequin and then through the bead. Then stick the point of the needle back through the sequin and the fabric. The bead holds the sequin in place.

To sew on ready-made lengths of sequins simply sew the threads that hold the sequins together on the underside onto the fabric with small stitches.

You can also make lines of sequins from individual ones. They should overlap like fish's scales to prevent the stitches showing. The method is as follows:
1. Bring the thread up through the fabric and through the first sequin which is placed flat on the fabric.
2. Sew into the fabric exactly at the edge of the sequin where the second sequin is to go. Bring the needle out again immediately alongside.
3. Now go back and take the needle and thread from above through the sequin and fabric. This sequin is now attached.
4 Now you can attach the next sequin by bringing the needle up through the fabric exactly where the double thread enters it at the edge of the first sequin.
5. Thread the new sequin onto the thread and place it on the fabric so

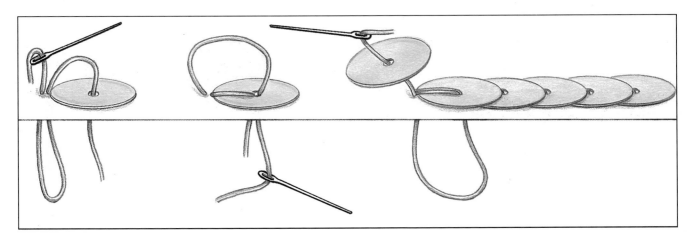

Making individual sequins into overlapping rows with concealed stitching.

that it half-covers the first sequin. Repeat step 2 and continue repeating the whole procedure until you reach the last sequin, which you can fix by using a small bead if you do not want the final stitch to show.

This method is used to build up lines of pattern, either straight or curved. But remember that just a few individual sequins can be extremely eye-catching for they contrast well with the fabric background.

Sewing on cord
Cord, which can be used in straight lines or ornamental designs on a fabric, or to outline small areas, can be simply oversewn with matching thread. To do this, bring the needle through the material underneath the cord, take the thread over the cord and stitch back into the fabric next to where the thread emerges. Continue in this way, keeping the stitches fairly close together.

With this method, however, the stitches are visible and may spoil the surface effect of the cord or appear untidy if they are not perfectly spaced. It is a better idea to take the thread through the bottom of the cord, and if you untwist the cord slightly with your free hand you can slip the needle through it easily enough.

Feathers and other materials
In appliquéing functional articles you must always bear in mind that they will have to be cleaned from time to time. Anything that will spoil in the wash or might damage the

background fabric during washing, must be sewn on in such a way that it can be easily removed. After washing it can then be sewn back into place.

Several feathers, for example, can be held together at the quill end with adhesive tape. If you leave a small opening in the appliqué hem, they can be pushed between the two layers of fabric. A few oversewn stitches will then hold the feathers in position.

Appliquéing with the sewing machine

Machine sewing is highly recommended for functional articles that will get a lot of wear and tear, and it is also much quicker. If you are to avoid making mistakes using this fast method and having to waste time unpicking your mistakes, it is a good idea to spend a little time preparing your work for sewing.

I particularly recommend that you use an iron-on backing. This can help, for instance, to make a flimsy background material more stable and, almost without exception, you will need it to strengthen the appliqué pieces themselves. If you use a backing, the pieces lie very flat and cannot crumple, and loose-weave fabrics keep their shape. By using white backing for light, semi-transparent fabrics, you will enable them to retain their own colour if used on a dark or patterned fabric, as the backing prevents the background colour showing through. (But if you want to retain the transparency of a fabric or of lace, you should of course not use the backing!) The backing will also prevent any hems showing on the right side.

You can manage basically with a one-sided iron-on backing. The double-sided backing, which makes it easier to fix appliqué sections onto the backing, is more expensive but it will save you having to pin or baste

these into position. Follow the manufacturer's instructions when ironing on the backing (not too hot) and do not move the iron from side to side. Simply apply pressure and the backing will not move.

Hemming and sewing on with straight stitch
With very fine fabrics such as silk or satin, you can turn under the edges of the appliqué sections (as for hand-sewn hemming stitch) and sew into place close to the edge with a thin matching thread. This is the best method if you do not want to emphasise the contours particularly. Proceed as follows:
1. Trace the contours of each piece of the appliqué motif separately on to one-sided backing and cut out the shape following the line exactly.
2. Place the backing on the wrong side of the appropriate fabric, put in a few pins if necessary and iron on.
3. Cut out the fabric allowing a $4\,mm/\frac{1}{8}$ in hem allowance all round.
4. As instructed for hand-sewn hemming stitch (see page 22), cut the hem allowance along curves and at corners, cutting not quite up to the backing.
5. Fold under the hem exactly along the edge of the backing. Pin or baste and iron the edge.
6. The appliqué section is now ready to be attached to the appropriate spot on the background. It should be pinned or basted and then machined into place with straight stitch close to the edge.

Tip:
If pins are placed perpendicular to the edge, you can machine over them. This will save you having to baste. But make sure that the appliqué piece lies completely flat so that no creases form behind it, for this can tend to happen with the 'pinning method'.

Appliquéing with zig-zag stitch

This method simultaneously overcasts and decorates the cut edges of the appliqué sections. The length of the zig-zag stitch is made so short that it makes a solid 'band' along the edge of the appliqué section and the finished effect resembles that of hand-sewn satin stitch (see page 22). Your choice of thread can create different colour effects. For example, you can work in the colour of the motif or the background fabric which makes the motif look correspondingly larger or smaller. Toning thread creates a harmonious effect, but a well chosen contrasting thread can be highly effective.

Remember that this stitch uses a lot of thread so make sure you always have enough of the colour you want. The lower thread can usually be an ordinary sewing thread of any colour, but adjust the tension on the machine so that it does not show on the right side. (For extra depth you can zig-zag stitch over an extra piece of thick thread laid along the seam line.)

The complete procedure for zig-zag stitch is shown in the photographs below. This simple, but effective, appliqué is used on the table linen on page 39.

1. Trace the outline of the appliqué section onto iron-on backing. (For a motif of several sections, trace each separately.) Cut out the shape following the line exactly. (See below.)
2. Place the backing on the wrong side of the appropriate fabric, put in a few pins if necessary and iron on.
3. Cut the fabric exactly along the edge of the backing for this method requires no hem allowance.
4. Attach the motif in the desired position on the background fabric. If you use double-sided backing it should be ironed on, otherwise it should be pinned (perpendicular to the edge) or basted.
5. To strengthen the stitching, sew first with straight stitch close to the edge. Sew as close to the edge as possible, for eventually, both the stitching and the cut edge must be hidden by the zig-zag stitching.
6. Set the zig-zag stitch length so short that it sews in a solid 'band'. The stitch should be wide enough to cover both the straight stitching and the edge. (For small sections do not make the stitching too wide or it will look rather cramped.) The machine needle enters alternately into the background fabric and then into the appliqué near the straight stitching.

Table mat with simple appliqué.

Tip:

If you can get used to taking all the thread ends through to the wrong side when you finish sewing and to knotting or casting them off, your appliqué will look much neater!

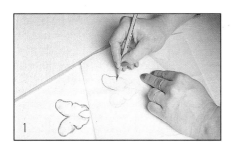

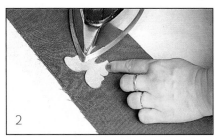

Creating a design

You are sitting there surrounded by heaps of fabric pieces, braids, lace, buttons, and so on – but where do you go from here? You can't think what to do and you are soon tempted to throw everything into a corner.

Don't do that! Try a more rational approach. Pick up the things that are lying around you and then go and look for a few ideas!

Motifs everywhere

Make your search for motifs a real experience. There are the flowers on the windowsill, the bunch of flowers on the dining-room table, the floral pattern on the living-room curtains, the geometric design on the carpet, the vegetable peelings in the kitchen, the tea-caddy with its beautiful lettering, the brightly printed paper bags from the nearby greengrocer, a child's drawing on the pinboard, the Art Nouveau bathroom tiles, the wallpaper in the bedroom, the photos from your last holiday, drawings in comics, children's books and magazines, and illustrations in cookery books. Go for a walk and you will find a variety of leaf shapes in the wood, pebbles by the stream and shells on the beach. In fact, there are subjects wherever you look, so that once more it is difficult to make up your mind.

One tip to get you started on your new hobby: begin with something very simple. With a ribbon appliqué for instance. Take a plain coloured shawl or cushion and decorate it with bright ribbons (see page 41). Or perhaps you are fed up with last summer's white flared skirt? A few pretty ribbons around the hem will give it a totally new look. You may even have enough time and materials to make a matching belt or T-shirt to complete your new outfit.

I hope this book will give you both ideas and practical help. Remember that neither functional nor decorative appliqué need be complicated and time-consuming. A simple design is often much more effective on an article of clothing or soft furnishing. Look for something you like, that won't prove too expensive and which you will enjoy making. Of course, you can feel free to elaborate on or simplify any of the ideas in this book. And you will soon come up with your own ideas.

Above: *A Tiffany mirror as a source of inspiration.*
Left: *A kitchen motif rich in contrast.*

Above: *A motif that can be made effectively in fabric and ribbon. Gift wrap can be a ready source of ideas!*

Opposite: *Cookery books – a feast for the eye . . .*

Right *. . . and origami too.*

Experimenting with shapes

I would like here to take a brief look at the various ways in which appliqué can be produced, namely how to find shapes or to invent your own. In the long run it is up to you whether you decide to take the easy or the more difficult path to the desired result – for the possibilities are endless with appliqué.

I am including only the main procedures in this section, as the various techniques come up repeatedly throughout the rest of the book where they are dealt with in more detail. For simplicity, I have divided the section roughly into two halves, beginning with the easiest techniques using ready-made shapes and leading onto the more complicated ones with your own motifs. There is, of course, no reason why you should not use any combination of these techniques.

Ready-made shapes in a new setting
Charming effects can be achieved with textile materials, with unusual items used out of context or parts of fabrics used elsewhere. Try taking such an item out of its usual setting and giving it a new use in an appliqué! But let's begin with something simpler.

A fabric with a pretty pattern which can be cut out and appliquéd.

Two lace motifs, each . . .

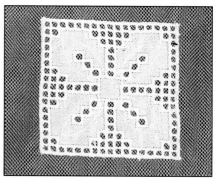

. . . appliquéd differently.

28

• Appliquéing *ribbons* in varying widths, colours and patterns, or *cords* is a very old and very simple technique. Experiment with braid, ric-rac, and straight and bias binding. Anything that will not fray can be sewn directly onto the fabric. You can use such materials to edge an article of clothing or a tablecloth, or you can use them to create a free linear pattern.

Remember that a wide braid (unlike cord) cannot follow a tight curve. Right angles and straight-edged geometric shapes will help to achieve the best result.

• In addition you can buy *ready-made embroidered motifs* which are very easy to appliqué and which have all the solidity of real embroidery. If you prefer you can combine these elements into a design of your own for a stunning effect.

• Haven't you often admired the *printed designs* on dressmaking or furnishing fabrics? An excellent way to use attractive designs is to cut out individual sections and use them as an eye-catching appliqué on toning plain fabric. You will find a stylish example of this in the cushion on page 42.

• If you can't find anything ready-made that you feel like cutting out, you can always reach for a pot of fabric paint or pen and *paint your own designs*. Children in particular will enjoy this, especially when a picture they have drawn eventually decorates a favourite T-shirt.

• Ready-made shapes can be found in all types of *lace*. You can use lace braid, whole doilies even, or beautiful single motifs cut out of curtains, tablecloths, petticoats, and so on. Recently, a range of lace has come on the market specially made for handicrafts and appliqué. You will find some ideas on how to use it on pages 54, 57 and 74/75 for both garments and soft furnishings.

• There are many *functional textile articles* which you can put to good use. Let your imagination run riot. Here are just a few of the things you could consider: handkerchiefs, tea-towels, ties, gauze bandage, orange nets, knitted gloves, oven-gloves and nylon tights.

• Any motif anywhere which inspires an appliqué can be *transferred* to a suitable textile. A pattern on tiles, for instance, or on a carpet, shapes in pictures or posters, on crockery or chocolate boxes – almost anything can be traced, and then reduced or enlarged to whatever size you require (see page 34).

Do not start with over-complicated shapes, many shapes can be simplified. You can decide whether to use the colours of the original or just to transfer the outline shape onto fabric, and whether you want to combine it with other shapes or develop it in some way. It is all purely a matter of personal taste.

A clever but practical appliqué made from painted fabric and baby socks.

Designing and combining motifs

It is particularly enjoyable to be able to turn motifs you have thought up yourself into reality with the aid of scissors and needle. Here the simplest of methods will often suffice, particularly in appliquéing finished articles. For textile pictures, especially representational ones, more complicated techniques will be necessary. First, a brief look at the possible ways of developing your own motifs.

• One idea is to *divide* an area in half by means of either a straight, zig-zag or curved line. The best way is to trace the line from your sketch onto cardboard, cut it out and then trace round it onto the appliqué fabric. You will first have to decide which half is to be in which fabric.

• Use the same method to include small *outline shapes* in your work. A cardboard template can, of course, be used over and over again so that the same motif can be used in a variety of different colours and patterns. Just remember that the more complicated the shape, the more difficult it will be to appliqué.

• With *positive-negative shapes* you can consciously bring out the interplay between motif and background. It is best to take the least striking fabric as the background. Where only a little of the background is exposed, it looks as if it has been inset, and this is known as fabric inlay. An interesting effect is achieved by combining appliquéd positive-negative sections into a patchwork design.

• A simple way of producing a balanced, symmetrical shape (see page 66) is to cut it from *folded paper*. Once you have managed to produce a pleasing paper pattern you can transfer it to fabric. This saves any irregularity (in folding and cutting bulky fabric) or any unpleasant shocks when you unfold the fabric.

• In an *exploded appliqué* scissors are again used to develop the design. Start by cutting a simple basic shape from paper or card, then cut this into several sections and separate them slightly. The original shape should still be recognisable. Once you are happy with the design on paper, transfer the separate sections to the

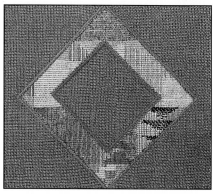

An interesting interplay of positive and negative shapes in two contrasting fabrics.

appliqué fabric (you can still make minor changes at this stage) and sew exactly as in the design.

• When designing, try cutting a piece of paper into several pieces. Cut the different pieces from different fabrics and butt them up to one another for appliquéing onto the background to give the impression of *patchwork*. A geometric design in particular will bring to mind a traditional patchwork quilt, but the technique can be just as effective with curved lines.

• In contrast to this butting technique, *overlapping the appliqué sections* can create depth. If, for instance, you want to portray a group of trees, begin with the trees at the back; the front trees can then overlap those at the back. Overlapping in this way is effective in making different parts of the design come forward or recede.

A simple curving line divides the surface in two.

A simple design made from folded paper. (You will find a more intricate example on page 66.)

With a detailed preliminary design you can save fabric on the hidden sections, leaving only a narrow border so that the cut edge of the lower section is completely concealed by the overlapping top shape.

● *Fabric pieces that stand away from the work* (with the edges first neatened of course) add solidity to the work in the same way as cords, feathers, and so on, especially when combined with the overlapping technique. You can also use padding under the entire appliqué or sections of it to give added body. Quilting can be used to give a gentle relief effect.

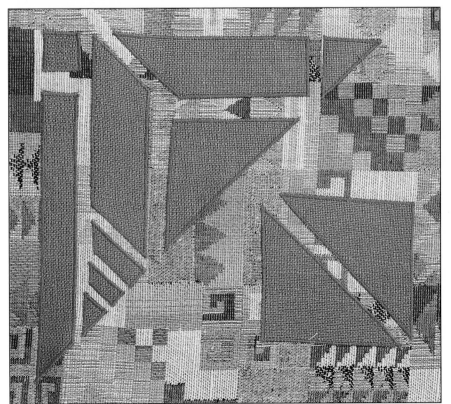

Top: *A geometric appliqué in patchwork style.*
Bottom: *An exploded appliqué.*

Pattern and colour

As well as considering the shapes in your appliqué work, much of your preparation should be devoted to collecting materials together. The final result will usually be better if you spend time choosing just the right fabric or combination, even if this involves dyeing a fabric, rather than if you rush into a compromise. Harmonious toning colours are essential for success. At the planning stage you can easily try any number of combinations, swopping certain colours or patterns around and adding new ones. Only when you are entirely satisfied with the choice of materials and colours, should you procede to the final designing, cutting and sewing.

This 'playing around' with the materials can produce good ideas of how to use them, so don't be afraid to change your ideas as you go along. The outcome will probably be better than if you had stuck to your original idea.

Whether you decide on a bright, richly contrasting appliqué with plenty of eye-catching pattern, or whether you prefer a quieter toning effect, depends not only on your personal preference, but also on its setting, that is on the style of the room or the article of clothing for which it is intended. There are, of course, no hard and fast rules, but experience has taught me a few things that you might like to bear in mind when developing your own designs. So here are some useful hints.

The effect of pattern

Remember that patterned fabrics often provide a focal point where none is intended. There is, of course, a great deal of difference between subdued textures and strong colour contrasts, between small and large patterns, between regular and irregular patterns, between slight and striking colour contrasts. In principle you can use any of these, but bear in mind that a fabric will look different on its own and when used with other fabrics. Make sure you test the effect in advance. You will make interesting discoveries!

In work where a feeling of depth and solidity is specially intended by the use of overlapping and colour, patterns can spoil the effect, making the work look flatter and destroying the illusion of depth.

This unusual appliqué gives an old mirror a new look. A light-coloured plain fabric in one colour only, sets off the different materials and contrasting shapes to good advantage. Soft feathers, hard shells, smooth and textured fabric, flat surfaces and strings of beads have been used. The subtle colouring makes the work suitable for use in a variety of different furnishing styles.

Colour in the home and in fashion

In the home simple, geometric appliqué designs go well with almost any style. A plain, restrained style of furnishing calls for intricate and striking designs, while a fussy or highly coloured furnishing style requires more careful harmonising of shape and colour. The appliqué should not be swallowed up by a 'loud' background.

If the work is to harmonise with its surroundings, the appliqué should always echo the main colours used in the room. If striking shapes in the room find an echo in the work, this will bring the appliqué and room together nicely. As we have already said, you might consider using the pattern of the carpet or curtains in a size suitable for the article you are making (see page 34).

Never hang an appliqué picture against a patterned wall. Decorative work is shown off to best advantage on a plain wall (this is true of any type of picture).

The so-called warm colours (red, orange, yellow and mixtures of these colours) are usually more striking and eye-catching than the cold, calm colours (green and blue and combinations of these).

When appliquéing on *clothing* the principle is the same. Remember that a little goes a long way! You wouldn't dream of using everything in your make-up bag every morning.

If you add an appliqué that is completely different from the article of clothing in both shape and colour, so there is no visual connection between them, it may look entirely out of place. Clothes 'decorated' in this way will often look worse than if you had left them as they were.

When giving a new look to an article of clothing, bear in mind what you might wear it with. Perhaps you can match shape or colour to this and so create an interesting overall effect.

Above: *A focal point on a long black coat is made with a colourful appliqué of feathers and embroidery.*

Right: *The motif need not be very large, for on a dark background contrasting colours are extremely eye-catching.*

Enlarging and reducing motifs

When you have found a motif that you want to use for an appliqué, it is a good idea to start by making a drawing on which you can base all the following stages of work (making templates, deciding on colours). Don't worry; you don't have to be Picasso!

Tracing a motif
Take a suitably sized sheet of tracing paper (or other transparent paper) and place it over the motif. Use a little adhesive tape to prevent it from moving. In this way you can copy pictures, embroidery motifs, photos and silk paintings, or patterns on tiles, carpets or crockery.

Simply trace the main outlines that you will use in your appliqué. At this stage you can still make changes, for it is not obligatory to copy the motif in every detail. It is quite likely that the traced motif will not be the right size for your appliqué, but it can be reduced or enlarged as appropriate.

If there is no photocopying shop nearby which can do this for you, change the size of the motif yourself by using the following method.

The grid method
The first step in this technique is to divide the preliminary drawing into equal squares. From this you can enlarge or reduce it or even change the proportions (for the latter, the squares of the second grid are replaced by rectangles, but this is an area I do not want to go into). Here, the method is explained by looking at how to enlarge your drawing.
1. Take the preliminary drawing that you want to enlarge and draw a grid of equally spaced horizontal and vertical lines over the drawing to divide it into squares. The distance between the lines will depend on the size of your drawing. For a small, complicated drawing the lines will have to be closer together than for a larger drawing.

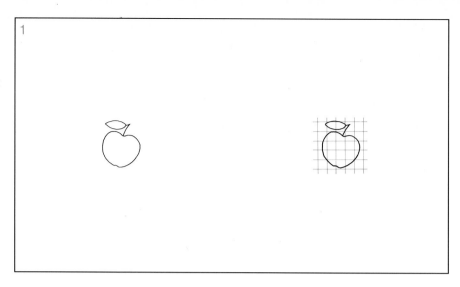

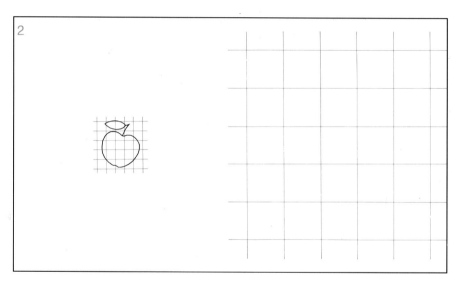

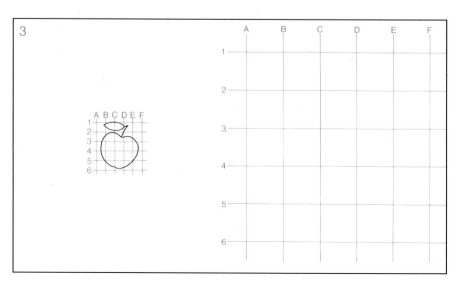

2. Measure the drawing and the area of the background fabric that the appliqué is to cover and work out by how much the drawing needs enlarging. You need to know this before you can draw your second larger grid. It should have exactly the same number of squares as the first one, the distance between the lines depending on how much it is to be enlarged. For example: the finished motif is to be four times as large as the original drawing. If the distance between the grid lines on the original drawing is $1\,\mathrm{cm}/\frac{2}{5}\,\mathrm{in}$, it will have to be $4\,\mathrm{cm}/1\frac{1}{2}\,\mathrm{in}$ in the second grid. When all the squares are added together, a grid $8\,\mathrm{cm}/3\frac{1}{8}\,\mathrm{in}$ wide will produce an area $32\,\mathrm{cm}/12\frac{1}{2}\,\mathrm{in}$ wide.

3. Next, mark all the horizontal and vertical lines on the first grid with letters and numerals so that it is easy to identify any point within the grid. Then mark the larger grid with the same letters and numerals. This will provide a check on whether you have the right number of lines and squares.

4. Now work your way around the outline of the drawing. Mark every point where it crosses a grid line with a small dot. All these points are transferred to the larger grid, using the letters and numerals as a guide.

5. Finally, join all the points together to create a new outline drawing. Compare your drawing continually with the original for small bends and curves cannot be well represented by the point method and need to be judged by eye.

You now have a larger drawing, but one in which all the proportions exactly match those of the original. This is the drawing you will now use for all further stages of work. (If you want to reduce a drawing, the distance between the lines in the second grid is reduced, but the method is the same in all other respects.)

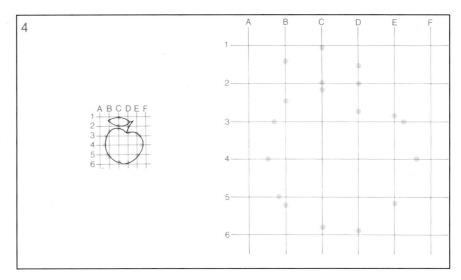

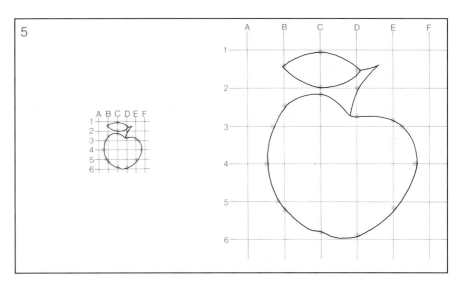

The five steps show how to set about enlarging any motif. To reduce a motif, the method is the same, but the new grid is made smaller.
Many of the motif ideas in this book are given in grid form so that you can set to work immediately.

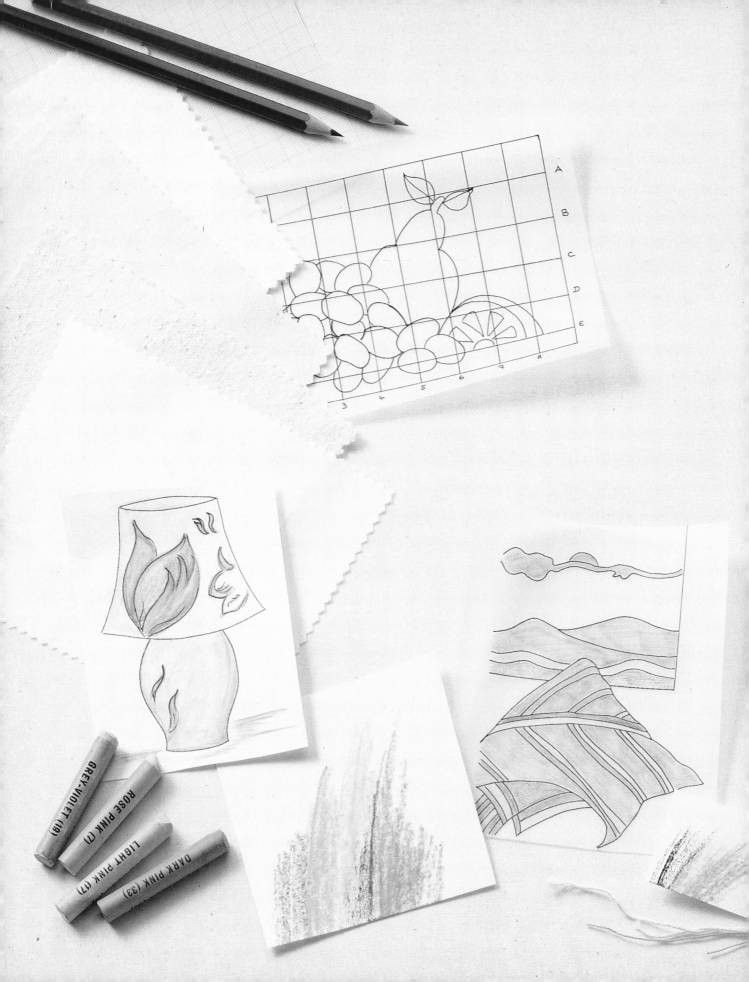

Home-furnishing and Fashion Ideas

Bordered butterfly tablecloth

You can give a really pretty look to a tablecloth with this simple appliqué. Since this is your first introduction to appliqué, the method is described in some detail. The colours and materials are designed to match the place-mats described earlier (see page 25). (If you have an artistic friend who can decorate your china with matching butterflies, your summer tea table will be complete!)

For the appliqué you will need the following materials:
- fabric remnant with several printed butterflies
- satin ribbon in two colours to match colours in the butterflies. The quantity will depend on the circumference of your tablecloth. The cloth used here measures 90 × 90 cm/35½ × 35½ in and requires around 3.60 metres/11¾ ft of each ribbon
- sewing thread to match the butterflies and ribbon
- iron-on backing

Ribboned hem
If you are decorating a tablecloth you already have, you can go straight on to sewing the ribbon evenly around the edge (step 6). But if you are making a new tablecloth you can combine the hemming with the appliqué and save yourself time and effort.

1. To position the outer satin ribbon 1 cm/⅖ in from the edge, first turn 1.5 cm/½ in of fabric over onto the right side all round the tablecloth and pin into position.

2. Iron around the edge and then open out the hem again. You will see a small square at each corner. Cut out a square slightly smaller than the one made by the lines.

3 Fold the two new corners down to make a triangle and to make a straight diagonal line across the corner. *Iron!*

4. Turn the hem down again. You can see now why it helps to have ironed it.

5. The horizontal corner line (which is only half its original length) now forms a neat join. Pin the corners and hem both sides evenly.

6. Pin the outer satin ribbon at an even distance from the edge (1 cm/⅖ in). (The cut edge or selvage of the tablecloth is concealed by the ribbon so that there is no need to turn it under or overcast it.)

Do not cut the ribbon at the corners but fold it neatly over. Excess ribbon disappears into a double-layered triangle and produces a diagonal line that should be exactly aligned with the corner of the cloth.

Using straight stitch, sew just inside the outer edge of the ribbon and then along the inner edge. The second ribbon can then be sewn into place, either a slight distance away from the first one or, as shown here, directly next to it. Appliquéd ribbon should not be washed or ironed at a high temperature as it shrinks!

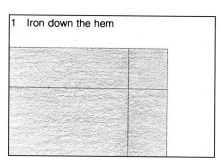

1 Iron down the hem

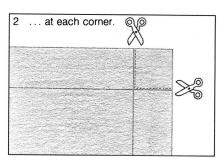

2 … at each corner.

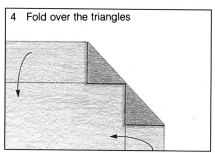

3 Cut out a square.

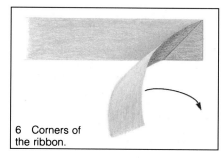

4 Fold over the triangles

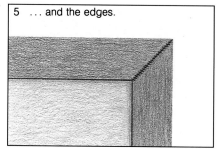

5 … and the edges.

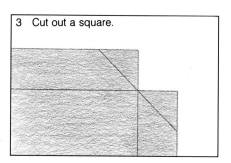

6 Corners of the ribbon.

Butterflies

Cut the butterflies out from the printed fabric remnant allowing a little extra fabric all round. Place them on the iron-on backing, draw around the outline and cut out. When all the butterflies have been reinforced on the wrong side with the backing (see page 24), cut more exactly around the butterfly. Arrange the motifs on the tablecloth. After pinning into position (or ironing with double-sided backing) sew into position with straight stitch just inside the edge and then oversew this with a short zig-zag stitch (see page 25).

You have already seen the placemat shown here on page 25. The ribbons appliquéd around the edge of the tablecloth match the colours in the butterflies.

The butterflies are cut from the fabric shown bottom left on page 28. It is, of course, impossible to cut out the small head and thin feelers, so these are embroidered in afterwards by hand or machine.

Beach towel for water babies

This fine-cotton appliqué is purposely confined to blue-green shades.

To make this unique beach towel, you need the following materials:

- a terry towelling bath towel
- plain-weave cotton fabric which will withstand 60°C/140°F wash in various blue and green shades
- dark, matching sewing thread
- iron-on, single or double-sided backing

For an appliqué with several different sections like this one, it is important to sew on the sections in the right order. The underwater plants that are partly covered by others will have to be pinned or ironed onto the towel first. For the fish, start with the head, fins and tail, and then, starting from the tail, add the scale sections (dark lines in drawing). When all these sections have been sewn into place, sew along the outline of individual scales with zig-zag stitch. Trace the separate sections of the motif onto iron-on backing in the usual way (see page 25). Remember that where the separate sections of the fish's body overlap, you should leave a little extra fabric on the underneath section to ensure that the towel cannot show through at the joins.

Below the design for the beach towel you will find a second idea: a water-lily motif. Many other designs are possible: shells, starfish, ducks, frogs, a swan, a rowing boat, a surfer, seagulls, and so on.

Cushion with geometric motif

Here we show you how to make a practical cushion cover, for it hardly seems worthwhile appliquéing a finished cushion. The cover uses the so-called 'hotel opening' so that it doesn't even need a zip.

You need the following materials:

- textured fabric (wild silk) measuring 92×43 cm/$36\frac{1}{4} \times 17$ in
- cotton remnant measuring 9×18 cm/$3\frac{1}{2} \times 7$ in
- matching ribbon (silk bias ribbon), in two lengths, 80 cm/$31\frac{1}{2}$ in and 115 cm/$45\frac{1}{4}$ in
- matching sewing thread
- iron-on backing

Reinforce two 9×9 cm/$3\frac{1}{2} \times 3\frac{1}{2}$ in squares (cotton) with iron-on backing. Make a narrow hem along one of the narrow sides of the cushion fabric and overcast the remaining sides with zig-zag stitch. Using diagram 1 as a guide, mark the front of the cushion, the centre line and centre point. Pin on the two squares and appliqué them, working outwards from the centre. Sew the first ribbon around the edge (see page 38). On the outer ribbon, the corners are emphasised by means of small 'cones'. When the appliqué is complete lay the fabric out (wrong side uppermost) and fold the narrow sides over one another, as shown in diagram 2. Sew together at each edge for 7 cm/$2\frac{3}{4}$ in. This makes a sort of tube. Turn it inside out (so that the appliqué is on the inside) and sew the side seams together (3). Iron. Turn the right way out – the cushion cover is finished!

Cushion covers with a 'hotel opening' (without zip) are very easy to make. First mark the front (40 × 40 cm/$15\frac{3}{4}$ × $15\frac{3}{4}$ in) and position the appliqué motif on this area.

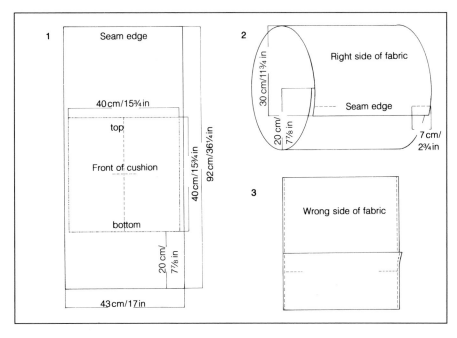

Pineapple cushion

At first glance this cushion motif looks much more complicated than it is. It was inspired by upholstering fabric left over from recovering an armchair. It is worth visiting a few upholsterers as they often have wonderful fabric remnants!

To make the cushion you need:

- slightly textured plain fabric
- remnant of furnishing fabric with large motif
- matching sewing thread
- iron-on backing

The cushion cover is made as shown on the previous page. The fabric is hemmed along one of the narrow sides and the other edges are over-cast with zig-zag stitch to prevent fraying. Mark the front of the cushion as shown in diagram 1 on page 41. Then cut out the chosen motif (allowing a little extra for thick upholstering fabric), place onto iron-on backing and draw round the outline. Cut out the backing shape and iron onto the back of the motif to reinforce it. Now you can cut the edges more exactly. Pin the motif onto the cushion-cover front and appliqué, first just inside the edge with straight stitch and then over-sewn with a short zig-zag stitch. For a neat effect, full of movement, try to follow the outlines exactly. Then make up the cushion cover as directed on the previous page.

Simple but effective: a single motif cut from a suitable furnishing fabric and appliquéd onto a cushion cover.

A new look for an old chair. A remnant of the upholstery fabric provides the appliqué for the cushion.

Relax amidst swathes of flowers

Here is another idea showing how you can use beautiful furnishing fabrics for a simple but striking appliqué. My antique Biedermeier sofa had been recovered with hand-woven linen. It had had several owners and the beautiful cover had a number of cigarette burns. As you know, reupholstering is expensive, so I decided to make a virtue out of necessity which resulted in the appliqué shown here. At an upholsterers I found a remnant of furnishing fabric with a beautiful Art Nouveau pattern. I decided to use a swathe of flowers as an appliqué for my sofa.

The project requires the following materials:

- flowered furnishing fabric
- iron-on backing
- fabric glue
- fine cotton cord
- sewing thread
- curved upholstery needle
- fabric paint (optional)

With an intricate motif like this it is not a good idea to cut it out and then

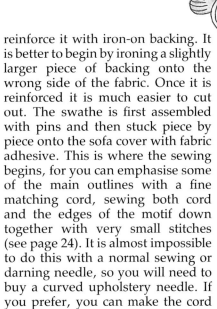

reinforce it with iron-on backing. It is better to begin by ironing a slightly larger piece of backing onto the wrong side of the fabric. Once it is reinforced it is much easier to cut out. The swathe is first assembled with pins and then stuck piece by piece onto the sofa cover with fabric adhesive. This is where the sewing begins, for you can emphasise some of the main outlines with a fine matching cord, sewing both cord and the edges of the motif down together with very small stitches (see page 24). It is almost impossible to do this with a normal sewing or darning needle, so you will need to buy a curved upholstery needle. If you prefer, you can make the cord

yourself from matching embroidery thread. Fine lines (for example, delicate flower stamens) can be painted in with fabric paint to complete the motif.

When the sofa again needs recovering you might like to try making your own inexpensive furnishing fabric (with appliqué, patchwork or silk-screen printing) which is used in the same way as a ready-bought fabric.

Here again a furnishing fabric motif makes an eye-catching appliqué. You could even appliqué a motif you have made yourself with fabric paint.

Appliquéd lampshade

The motif for this lamp was inspired by a cushion cover whose pattern included a number of wavy lines. This design harmonises well with the circular lamp-base and the panelled effect of the shade.

You will need the following materials:

- fabric in three colours (to tone with the lamp and furnishings)
- double-sided iron-on backing
- matching cord
- fabric glue
- sequins (optional)

Make a paper template from one panel of the lampshade. Use a second piece of paper to design the template for the waves. You will need only one, for by moving it slightly you can cut three different sizes of iron-on backing. Iron the backing onto the fabric and cut round the edge. Starting with the largest underneath piece, iron the pieces (not too hot, wool setting) onto the lampshade. Emphasise the edges by gluing on cord. A few sequins can be used to create a focal point.

A clever (adhesive) motif for a lamp by day . . .

. . . and by night.

Curtain for French window

A plain curtain can be transformed into a decorative item that will bring a breath of summer into the room. Find an interesting piece of lace panel; its size will determine the size of the fabric surround. Materials:

- a light-coloured curtain (it is quick to make on net or sheer curtains)
- a piece of lace panel or curtain
- natural-coloured cotton
- sewing thread
- fabric paint
- fabric flowers (optional)

After working out the measurements (stick more or less to the proportions shown in the photograph) and cutting the strips for the 'window frame', start by pinning the lace into position. When you sew on the strips (with straight stitch along a turned under hem) you can sew the lace at the same time. Small triangles are used to decorate the 'frame' or make the 'door handle'. A monogram is added at the centre.

The flower pot is painted, cut out and appliquéd separately. It can be made to look more real with separate overlapping leaves or fabric flowers.

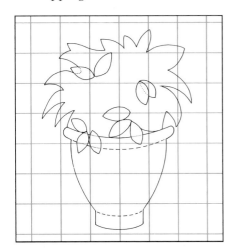

The design for the flower pot.

This appliqué is extremely effective on a light fabric.

A chair and . . .

A chair needed recovering; I decided on a co-ordinated effect to give the mirror a new look too.

You need the following materials:

- plain, light-coloured furnishing fabric for the seat cover
- foam
- upholstery tacks
- 1 m/3¼ ft gros grain or heavy brocade (4 cm/1½ in wide), brown
- striped furnishing fabric
- brown sewing thread

Measure the area of the seat, adding several centimetres or inches to your measurement to allow for the thickness of the foam and for the hem; cut out the light fabric. On the right side, mark two lines crossing at the centre to position the square motif.

Cut the gros grain or brocade into five strips of 20 cm/7¾ in length and cut the furnishing fabric into five similar patterned strips of 20 cm/7¾ in length, but of varying widths according to the pattern. Placed side by side they should give a total width of 20 cm/7¾ in so that they will eventually make a square. Now interweave the two sets of strips with the gros grain or brocade going in one direction and the patterned strips in the other. Push them all close together to form a 20 × 20 cm/7¾ × 7¾ in square. Pin them together. Once you have the square pinned correctly onto the chair covering (using the marked lines as a guide) you can machine along all the edges. Edges of the gros grain or brocade can be sewn with straight stitch but the patterned strips need sewing with a short zig-zag stitch.

Finally, cut a few triangles from the patterned fabric and sew here and there onto the gros grain or brocade to break up the design. Use the appliqué to recover the seat of the chair using the foam and the upholstery tacks.

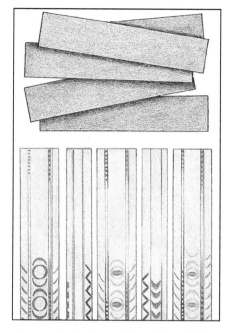

Gros grain (or brocade) and furnishing fabric strips are interwoven.

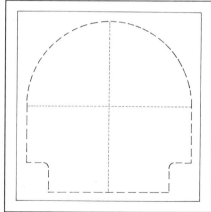

Above: *Whatever the shape of your chair seat, mark the outline and the centre lines. Leave enough all round to allow for a generous hem.*

Left: *A close-up of the woven strips with additional appliquéd triangles.*

... a mirror with a new look

From a distance the appliqué gives this mirror an Italian Renaissance look. It works best on a frame that is wide, but not too thick, and is also easiest to do. Materials:

- dark-brown furnishing fabric, velvet or leather
- border cut from furnishing fabric or ready-bought braid (narrower than frame)
- sewing thread
- adhesive tape
- small glazing nails

Lay the frame (with mirror removed) on the right side of the brown material and mark exactly along the outside and inside edges, taking special care at the corners. Allow an extra $3\,cm/1\frac{1}{4}$ in both outside and inside (more for a thicker frame) and cut out this wide, fabric frame.

Sew the border all around the fabric frame inside the marked lines. Borders with selvages can be sewn with a simple straight stitch. Add small rectangles, the same width as the border, at the corners.

When you have finished the appliqué, cut diagonally through the extra allowance at the inside corners stopping just short of the marked line. When you pull the fabric over the frame you can turn it under slightly at this point. Small glazing nails help hold the inner corners secure. Treat the outer corners in the same way (but without cutting into excess fabric). On the back of the frame, the edges of the fabric are secured with a few stitches and stuck down with adhesive tape. Replace the mirror in the frame and there is your new-look mirror!

An old chair gets a new seat cover, and a mirror a new frame.

A picture for the kitchen

This easy-to-make picture was inspired by my neighbour's patent cure for headaches: the juice of half a lemon squeezed into a cup of coffee. After drinking it you will soon find that your headache has gone! Here then is how you go about making the picture.

For a 30 × 40 cm/11¾ × 15¾ in picture you will need:

- brown fabric (hessian; 34 × 16 cm/ 13¼ × 6⅓ in)
- light-coloured fabric (twill; 34 × 30 cm/13¼ × 11¾ in)
- dark brown lining satin for the coffee pot (roughly 25 × 25 cm/10 × 10 in)
- one piece each yellow, white and green lining satin
- iron-on backing
- sewing thread in matching shades

First make the background. Place the two pieces of fabric right sides together so that two of the 34 cm/ 13¼ in edges lie together. Sew a straight seam (1) 1 cm/⅖ in from the edge, open out the fabric and iron the seam flat to give the completed two-tone background (2). (It can be seen as representing a tabletop and the wall behind it.)

This is basically the first stage in the patchwork technique, for as you can imagine, an appliqué background could be made much more intricate by sewing a number of fabric pieces together in this way (3). Whichever way the seams run – whether diagonal, horizontal or vertical – they must always be sewn very carefully to avoid the fabric puckering. Bear in mind, however, that a background for an appliqué should not be too fussy for it should not draw the eye away from the appliqué nor spoil its effect.

To return to our picture. Enlarge the motif design to the required size (30 × 40 cm/11¾ × 15¾ in). Trace the separate shapes onto paper and cut out. Use this as a template to cut the iron-on backing exactly to size. Iron these pieces onto the correct fabric. Cut out following the outside edge precisely and pin (or iron, if you are using double-sided backing) in place on the background. Sew all the pieces first with straight stitch close to the edge and then oversew with a short zig-zag stitch in the appropriate colour thread (see page 25). Do not worry about sewing round the light-coloured lid with dark thread, for this helps it stand out better from the background.

If you are going to frame the picture (after first mounting the appliqué on cardboard) why not paint the frame to match your picture? I have used yellow here, for by using one of the colours in the appliqué the whole thing holds together better.

Appliqué pictures can also be made as wall hangings. For this you should first make a narrow hem along both sides and at the bottom. The top hem, which will be wider than the others, is sewn last. A wooden batten is pushed through this seam and the hanging suspended from it.

Where can you find ideas for other designs? I have included a second design here. Perhaps you can find a piece of check material for the tablecloth, and the asparagus tips can be carefully coloured in with green fabric paint. You can find a lot of other ideas in magazines, advertisements, catalogues, packaging – and of course in your own cooking. Always be on the lookout for new ideas!

Far left: A simple seam joins the two pieces of fabric that make the background (1 and 2).

Alongside: By dividing up the area with straight lines more intricate backgrounds can be made in patchwork style (3).

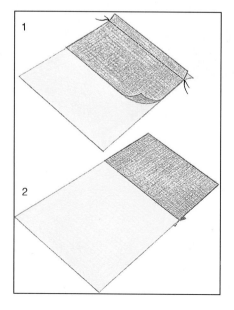

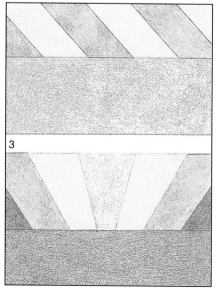

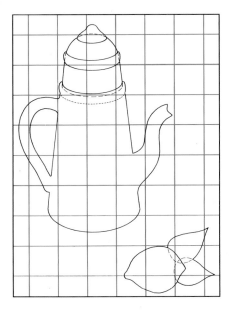

In this preliminary drawing for the kitchen picture illustrated alongside, the lines of dashes show which sections overlap. The dotted line indicates a final line of stitching.

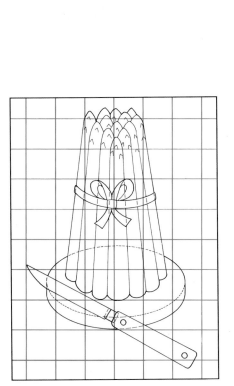

The two-tone background for the picture is made first. The colour of the frame is chosen to echo one of the colours in the picture.

A second suggestion for a kitchen picture: the asparagus stalks are best made from one piece of fabric. Before appliquéing the ribbon, add all vertical lines by machine.

Let the children join in

Do you have a son or daughter who comes and peers inquiringly over your shoulder when you are appliquéing? If you have, you will like this suggestion, for it is one children can help with. Denim jackets are a favourite with children of all ages, and it is more than likely that your son or daughter will have one, or, if not, you could look out for one at a jumble sale or charity shop. Why not turn this denim jacket into a unique article of clothing?

I got the idea for this design when I received an airmail letter, and remembered how much children like letters.

You will need:

- white cotton (about 20 × 15 cm/ 7¾ × 6 in)
- red and blue cotton border (1 m/ 3¼ ft each)
- red, white and blue sewing thread
- iron-on backing (optional)
- fabric pens and paints

Above: *A unique denim jacket.*

Right: *A T-shirt with boat motif.*

Below: *A positive-negative monogram.*

If the cotton is not very thick, cut a piece of backing to the size of the 'letter' and iron onto the fabric. Then cut out the letter shape, adding a seam allowance of 0.5 cm/⅕ in all round which you turn over and iron down onto the wrong side.

Appliqué on the red and blue stripes at regular intervals. They should be cut 1.5 cm/½ in long each with a similar diagonal cut. Then with the fabric pen or paint you could write in the child's name and address or, for safety, the address of a dream holiday spot, like a theme park, and add an attractive stamp and postmark. If your child happens to have a toy post office set which includes a postmark stamp, this will provide an authentic touch (use fabric paint with it).

When the envelope is finished it should be sewn close to the edge with straight stitch to the back of the jacket.

Another idea is to decorate the jacket with the child's initials in a positive-negative design. This fabric inlay technique is briefly described on page 30.

You will need:

- two toning pieces of cotton, one of them could be patterned
- matching sewing thread
- iron-on backing

Decide on the size of the design and how it is to be divided up, and cut a piece the size of the complete design in the fabric that is to go underneath. A piece of backing exactly half this size should be ironed onto the second fabric and cut out. Now sketch the mirror image of the two letters onto the backing and cut out exactly with sharp scissors. The remaining piece of fabric is placed over half the background (to form the negative). The two letters that have been cut out are placed on the other half. Sew firmly into place along all edges (see page 25) and then sew the whole design into place on the article of clothing.

The other illustrations here show that it is possible to cut out and appliqué children's drawings. This prevents possibly ruining a T-shirt by painting directly onto it.

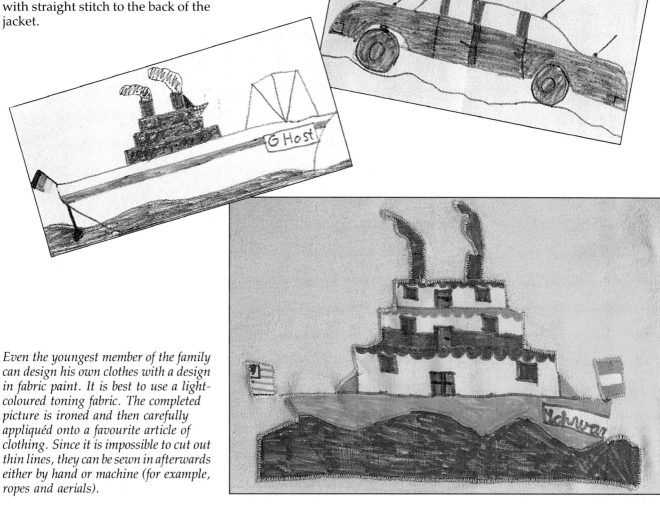

Even the youngest member of the family can design his own clothes with a design in fabric paint. It is best to use a light-coloured toning fabric. The completed picture is ironed and then carefully appliquéd onto a favourite article of clothing. Since it is impossible to cut out thin lines, they can be sewn in afterwards either by hand or machine (for example, ropes and aerials).

A shirt – bold and cheeky

A poster inspired this design. The graphic techniques that use areas of bold colour, especially those of Pop Art posters, are an ideal basis for appliqué. I started by sketching a detail of the poster (see below), and making a few changes in the process. The final appliqué design incorporates several elements from the poster.

The basis for the design is a man's shirt. Carefully unpick the collar, cut it in half and neaten the cut edges (by turning under a small hem). Sew the collar back onto the shirt with the original front points now at the back and the other (new) points now at the front. Now the shirt is ready to be appliquéd.

You will need:
- thin cotton (or satin) in red (about 40 × 40 cm/15¾ × 15¾ in), yellow (about 65 × 25 cm/25½ × 10 in) and other bright colours for the sleeve decoration
- 50 cm/19¾ in dark blue cord
- 4 dark blue buttons, 1 tie
- matching sewing thread

In choosing the appliqué fabrics it is very important that they should be no thicker than the fabric of the shirt itself, for this would tend to stop the appliqué hanging properly. It is better not to use iron-on backing so that the fabric will fall softly. You should therefore begin by turning under a narrow hem (ironing it down before sewing) on all sections of the appliqué before sewing it into place close to the edge with straight stitch.

Following the diagram below, first

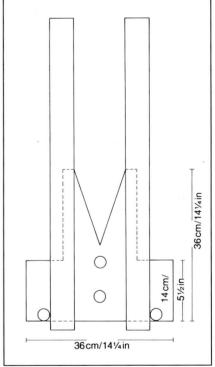

Design and cutting plan for the appliqué.

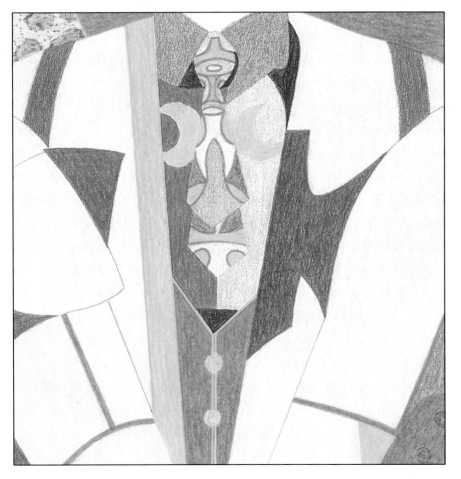

The length of the bold and cheeky design depends on the length of the shirt.

cut out the red waistcoat section and the yellow strips. You can alter the length of the yellow strips to fit the length of the shirt. Turn under a hem all round (except where the broken lines indicate that the edge will be concealed) and sew the waistcoat section onto the back of the shirt, starting roughly 10 cm/4 in above the bottom edge. Over this, appliqué the two yellow strips up as far as the shoulder yoke and down to slightly beyond the base of the waistcoat, so that they cover the top points of the waistcoat and separate the centre part of the waistcoat from the side 'pockets'. The pockets are outlined in dark blue cord (see page 24) and the four buttons are sewn into place. Now all you need is the tie. Tie it in the usual way, cut the loop that goes round the neck exactly in half and sew the two ends into place at the front, right and left under the collar.

You need not restrict the bold colours to the back of the shirt; you can cut strips and rectangles from the other colours of fabric and appliqué them diagonally onto the sleeves. You may find this difficult to do with the sewing machine, but it will not take long to appliqué the sleeves by hand. Leave the front of the shirt fairly plain; a few bold triangles of colour on the breast pocket would be enough.

Naturally you can make this design in other colours, and it does not have to be done on a plain white shirt. But if you choose to do it on a checked shirt you might find that the appliqué loses some of its boldness, for this is largely dependent on the contrast of the bright colours with the white. How about trying the same design on a plain black shirt!

A colourful poster inspired this witty design for a shirt. The collar is removed, cut in half and replaced back to front before beginning the appliqué.

Knitting and lace

Lace appliqué is really effective on a plain article of clothing and where it tones well it can form a subtle focal point. Here is a suggestion for anyone who wants to add style to a plain cardigan.

You will need:

- a pretty motif cut from a lace curtain
- matching beads
- sewing thread

After carefully cutting the motif out of the curtain, pin it, or better still, roughly baste it to the cardigan. It is important not to stretch the cardigan as you sew or the appliqué will not lie flat. Sew all round the edge by hand with a close-set satin stitch. If you would prefer the areas of thin tulle in the lace to remain transparent, first sew all round them with a close satin stitch (making sure you sew through both the lace and the knitted surface beneath) to prevent fraying. Then, from the wrong side, carefully cut away the knitted sections enclosed by these sewing lines, leaving just the tulle in place. As a final touch, sew a few small beads onto the lace, for example into the centres of flowers – and your cardigan is complete.

Another idea is to combine knitting with knitting. If you want to use part of an old sweater, first reinforce the section with iron-on backing, cut it out, oversew with zig-zag stitch and then appliqué wherever required.

The lace motif on this cardigan came from a lace curtain. The slight colour contrast focuses the eye on the different fabric structures.

A draw-string evening bag

Perhaps you need a bag for an evening at the theatre. You can make yourself one fairly quickly. You will want to choose the colour and fabric to match your outfit, so the idea shown here, as with those elsewhere in the book, is only a suggestion.

You will need:

- velvet remnant (about 35 × 50 cm/ 13¾ × 19¾ in)
- matching lining (50 × 7 cm/19¾ × 2¾ in)
- about 1.50 m/5 ft gold braid (make sure it bends easily)
- 1 packet sequins
- about 60 cm/23¾ in matching velvet ribbon
- sewing thread

Cut out the velvet as shown in the diagram (oversew the edges with zig-zag stitch) and appliqué on the braid and sequins. You can either follow the design shown or invent one of your own. The only thing to remember is that the braid must start and finish the same distance from the top edge, so that the two ends meet exactly when the bag is sewn up. Then sew on the lining strip (right sides together, iron the seam flat) and, working in one continuous procedure, sew together sides a, then b and finally c, d and e. Fold in the lining strip and, 3 cm/1¼ in below the top edge, make a line of straight stitches. Put in a second row 1.5 cm/½ in below the first to make a channel through which to thread the velvet ribbon. (You will need to unpick the side seam slightly to thread the ribbon through.) Your new evening bag is complete.

Alongside the cutting guide for the bag with a design idea (gold braid and sequins) is a diagram showing the order in which the seams should be joined.

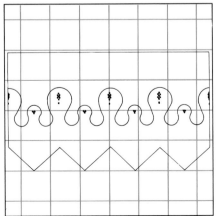

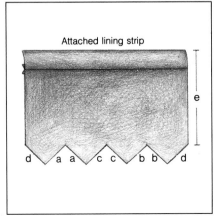

Attached lining strip

Stylish cardigan

An easy way of giving an individual look to a knitted cardigan is to add an appliqué of geometric shapes, preferably in a matching colour. Make the appliqués as directed and then sew them on by hand. This will make them easier to remove when required and the knitting is less likely to stretch (than with machine sewing).

You will need:

- cotton satin in the same colour as the cardigan
- matching sewing thread
- iron-on backing

Measure the distance between the shoulder seam and the beginning of the buttonholes. Cut a strip of paper 2 cm/¾ in wide to this length and on it construct three 'hollow' triangles, of the same base length but different heights. Cut the ends of the strip to a point. Transfer the outline of the design to iron-on backing, cut out and iron onto the wrong side of the satin. Place a second piece of satin under it (right sides together) and pin, then adding 0.5 cm/³⁄₁₀ in seam allowance all round, cut out the outline. Following the edge of the backing, sew the two layers of satin together along the pointed sides of the triangles. Turn the satin the right way out, pushing out all corners and seams, and then sew all the way round (including the straight edge this time) close to the edge with straight stitch. Now sew around the inner triangles, cut them out and oversew with zig-zag stitch. Sew both the strip and the triangle cut-outs to the cardigan by hand.

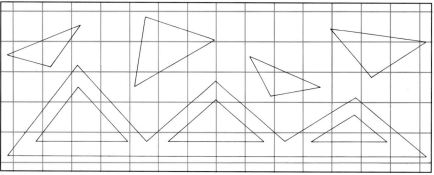

A design idea for the appliqué. The length of the zig-zag strip should be the same as that of the neck edge of the cardigan.

Granny's old lace doily

If you are lucky enough to have two doilies the same, you can do as I have done and use them to decorate the sleeves of a blouse. I used them on a sleeveless blouse to which I wanted to add sleeves.

You will need:

- 2 small white lace doilies
- white cotton (about 50×90 cm/ $19\frac{3}{4} \times 35\frac{1}{2}$ in) if you need to make sleeves
- white sewing thread
- white beads (optional)

First cut the fabric for the sleeves if appropriate. You can make them fairly wide by gathering or pleating the top. Before sewing up the sleeves, pin on the lace doilies and pin up the sleeves just to see how they lie. Then appliqué on the lace with zig-zag stitch, sew up the sleeves and set them into the blouse. A few beads add to the effect. (If you are using a blouse that already has sleeves, sew on the appliqué by hand.)

You can make a see-through lace appliqué if you first sew close to the edge of the lace with straight stitch. Then on the wrong side cut away the cotton leaving 2 mm/$\frac{1}{10}$ in inside the line of stitching and, using a close zig-zag stitch, sew all round the edge (to cover both the straight stitching and the edge of the cotton fabric).

Why not consider dyeing both the blouse and the lace in an interesting new colour?

A self-coloured design: the pale colours show off the structure of the lace to good effect. In the blouse illustrated the fabric has been left beneath the lace.

Fur – a real eye-catcher

Here the seams on a black sweatshirt inspired a fur appliqué. The fluffiness of the materials almost conceals the fact that the motif has been woven.

You will need:

- 8 strips of different fur (off-cuts from a furrier)
- about 1 m/3¼ ft black gros grain or heavy brocade (2 cm/¾ in wide)
- a little black leather
- black sewing thread

Cut four of the shorter strips of fur to the same length; the others should be longer and vary in length. Interweave all the strips of fur (short and long alternately) with three lengths of gros grain or brocade so that the gros grain conceals the ends of the shorter strips. Arrange on the sweatshirt, pin into position and sew on the gros grain close to the edge. It is now impossible for the strips of fur to come free although the eight ends of the longer strips are still free. Hold each in place with a small triangle of leather.

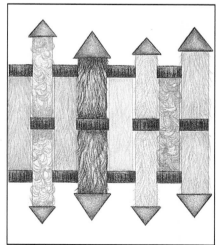

Different furs of varying lengths are interwoven with gros grain.

How to weave the appliqué.

Perching butterflies

This jacket made in a Mexican curtaining fabric, richly scattered with flowers, gave me the idea of completing the effect with a few feather butterflies.

You will need:

- feather butterflies (available from flower or soft-furnishing shops)
- a little dark-coloured leather
- dark sewing thread
- adhesive

The butterflies are glued onto the leather and then the leather is cut out following the shape of the butterflies, but with an additional 1.5 cm/½ in all round. Now all you need to do is to sew them on where required. Make sure you take them off before having the jacket cleaned. Don't sew the butterflies on too flat, they should perch on the flowers!

The leather will look less out of place if you use a little leather elsewhere on the jacket. In the jacket illustrated a leather trim was added at the sleeve seam.

A butterfly on your shoulder.

Only a few butterflies need to be appliquéd to a richly patterned jacket.

Suede blouson with fabric trim

Furnishing fabric can give an old suede jacket a new look. Materials:

- matching leather remnants
- striped furnishing fabric
- matching sewing thread

Make a paper pattern of the top section of the back of the jacket and a similar pattern for the front. The pattern for the front should form a triangle from the outside of the shoulder seam to the bottom of the front fastening. Adding a seam allowance, cut the furnishing fabric from these patterns and appliqué with strips of leather. Unpick the collar, shoulder and back sleeve seams and sew together again to catch in the appliqué. At the front, secure the appliqué along the front fastening only. The appliqué should remain free along the front diagonals and along the bottom of the back panel.

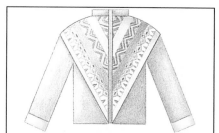

Leather strips are appliquéd to toning furnishing fabric. New front and back yoke panels give an old suede blouson a new look.

For the front cut the furnishing fabric so that the stripe runs parallel to the diagonal side edge. The leather strips should also be attached diagonally at regular intervals (diagram). On the back yoke (small photo) pattern and strips run horizontally.

The leopard has escaped

Here once more, as in the cushion on page 42, the motifs have been taken from a printed fabric. At first glance, the appliqué looks much more complicated than it is.

You will need:

- motifs from printed fabric
- matching sewing thread
- iron-on backing
- glass eyes (available from handicraft shops)

First, roughly cut out the motifs and iron the backing onto the wrong side. Then cut exactly around the outline of the motif and sew onto the sweatshirt. Sew close to the edge with straight stitch then oversew with a short zig-zag stitch (see page 25). Secure the eyes on the wrong side through the wire loop.

At a time when safari styles are fashionable you will find a lot of fabrics with wild animal motifs. Here a leopard is used, cut from a printed fabric and appliquéd on.

The close-up photograph clearly shows the glass eyes. Fine lines (for example, whiskers) are best embroidered by hand or machine. You can use the same technique to emphasise other lines within the appliqué or to embroider whole areas to change their colour (for example, nose, ears, outline of head).

Suede bag and waistcoat

To finish with, another idea that combines suede with furnishing fabric. For the *bag* you will need:

- suede (about 50 × 70 cm/19¾ × 27½ in)
- suede and furnishing fabric remnants for the appliqué
- a few feathers
- 2 metal rings for the shoulder strap
- matching sewing thread

From the suede cut the gusset, the shoulder strap and the binding strips, cutting one of each pattern piece, and then three of the main bag section (for front, back and flap). Sew the front to the back with the gusset strip between them (working on the right side). Extend the gusset strip 6 cm/2⅓ in either side to make loops to hold the metal rings. Use a paper template to help you cut the leather and fabric strips for the

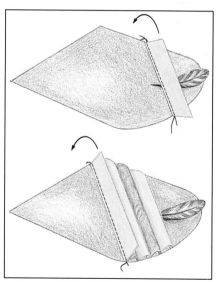

Each strip is sewn on right sides together and then folded back. The second edge of each strip is sewn at the same time as the following strip is attached.

Shoulder strap		6 cm/2⅜ in
	120 cm/47¼ in	
Binding strips		
		3 × 20 cm/ 7⅞ in
	60 cm/23⅝ in	
Gusset	5 cm/2 in	
	72 cm/28⅜ in	

Back, front, flap

3 ×   20 cm/7⅞ in

Paper template for the appliqué strips

20 cm/7⅞ in

appliqué and do not forget to add a seam allowance. Then sew them strip by strip onto the flap of the bag as shown in the diagram, beginning at the bottom corner and remembering to catch the feathers into the first seam. Trim the edges, and sew the flap onto the back of the bag (on the wrong side), then bind all seams and the edges of the flap with the narrow suede strips.

Sew the shoulder strap double and fasten it to the metal rings.

For the *waistcoat* start by making a proper pattern and use it to restyle an old suede jacket. The key to the whole design is the interwoven appliqué on the front and shoulder yoke. You will need:

- about 5 m/16½ ft dark brown gros grain or heavy brocade (6 cm/ 2⅓ in wide)
- strips of patterned furnishing fabric (3 cm/1¼ in wide)
- strips of suede (3 cm/1¼ in wide)
- matching sewing thread

Neaten the edges of the fabric strips with zig-zag stitch and sew the gros grain or brocade together to halve its width.

Use a paper pattern to cut out the waistcoat sections. (If your jacket has back seams make sure you centre the pattern exactly. You might like to add a matching half-belt.) First sew the shoulder seams together and leave the side seams open for the time being. Starting from the point at the bottom of the front, cover the front with strips, alternating between suede, gros grain and fabric. Make both fronts symmetrical. All the strips will need to extend slightly beyond the edge of the waistcoat for when woven they will be shorter. Then, working in exactly the same order on both fronts, interweave the remaining strips diagonally with the first ones. Push the whole thing together firmly and pin the edges.

A strip of suede is sewn down the centre of the shoulder yoke and the edge of the yoke trimmed in the same way. Trim the strips all around the edge, sew up the side seams and bind all edges with strips of leather.

Right: *Enlarge the pattern pieces to fit your size.*

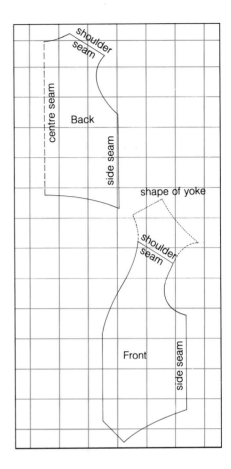

Above: *The woven shoulder yoke.*
Right: *Before sewing up the side seams, the strips are laid out, interwoven and then sewn and trimmed around the edges.*

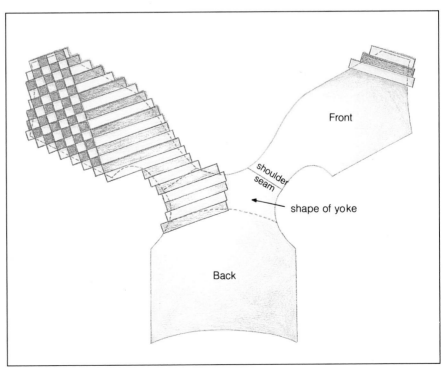

Waterside castle, Büdingen
(Anita Geldner)

Monreal village scene (Anita Geldner)

King of Hearts (Anita Geldner)

Appliqué Gallery

Palace garden impressions (Anita Geldner)

Hawaiian appliqué (Doris Winter)

Crazy appliqué (Doris Winter)

I love tulip fields (Doris Winter)

Quilt (Amanda Lehmann)

School class (Ursula Ahrens)

Family christening (Ursula Ahrens)

Above: *Dolls' house (Gertrud Schupp)*

Right: *Art Nouveau house (Gertrud Schupp)*

Vase of flowers (Helga Westphal)

Town of Latium (Helga Westphal)

Hannover (Bianca Methe)

Little Venice (Bianca Methe)

Spring (Monique Graf)

Papageno (Monique Graf)

Author's Acknowledgments
Sincere thanks to dressmakers Mrs Bucher and Mrs Hartl for their help in making some of the items in this book, and to Myra Davidson for making the machine sewn appliqué on page 16.

Illustration Acknowledgments
Photographs: Bayerische Verwaltung der staatlichen Schlösser, Gärten und Seen, Munich p. 15; BLV Verlagsgesellschaft GmbH, Munich pp. 72, 73; Foto-Design-Studio Gerhard Burock, Wiesbaden-Naured pp. 6–7, 18, 19, 27 (top right, bottom left and right), 36–7, 64–5 (background), 74, 75; Alexander Graf, Montreux pp. 78, 79; The Hamlyn Publishing Group, London – David Johnson p. 16; Claus Hansmann, Stockdorf pp. 10, 11, 12, 13, 14, 69, 70, 71; Hans-Jörg Hennig AWI, Heidelberg pp. 66, 67, 68; Photo-Atelier A. Löhr, Bendorf/Rhein pp. 64–5; Hans Starosta, Studio für Fotografie, Göttingen pp. 76, 77; Christa Thoma, Friedrichschafen pp. 1, 2, 3, 9, 17, 21, 25, 28, 29, 30, 31, 32, 33, 39, 40, 41, 42, 43, 44, 45, 46, 47, 49, 50, 51, 53, 54, 55, 56, 57, 58, 59, 60, 61, 62, 63; TLC-Foto-Studio GmbH, Bocholt pp. 26, 27 (top left).
Line drawings: Brigitte and Rolf Dähler, Bad Schwalbach

First published 1988 by
The Hamlyn Publishing Group,
Michelin House,
81 Fulham Road,
London SW3 6RB.

First impression 1988

Published in the U.S.A. by
Stackpole Books
Cameron and Kelker Sts.
Harrisburg, PA 17105

Reprinted 1989

Typeset by J&L Composition Ltd, Filey, North Yorkshire
Printed by Mandarin Offset, Hong Kong

Library of Congress Card Number 89–21812
ISBN 0–8117–2310–0